Overview of the Markets

OVERVIEW OF THE MARKETS

Brian Coyle

FINANCIAL
WQRLD
Publishing
THE CHARTERED INSTITUTE OF BANKERS

Financial World Publishing
IFS House
4-9 Burgate Lane
Canterbury
Kent
CT1 2XJ
United Kingdom

Telephone: 01227 818687

Financial World Publishing publications are published by
The Chartered Institute of Bankers, a non-profit making registered educational charity.

Typeset by Kevin O'Connor
Printed in Italy

ISBN 0-85297-452-3

Contents

Introducing the Capital Markets

A company wishing to raise long-term finance, from sources other than retained profits, will try to do so in the capital markets, or by borrowing long-term from a bank or syndicate of banks. Therefore company managers need to have an understanding of the markets, and the purpose of this book is to present an overview of what they are, and their main characteristics.

The Financial Markets

In the financial markets, securities and other financial instruments, and money itself, are bought and sold, or borrowed and lent. Financial markets can be categorized into three broad groups:

- the capital markets, consisting primarily of the equity markets and bond markets that are for medium-term to long-term financial instruments and loans
- the money markets that are for short-term financial instruments and loans
- the foreign exchange markets (FX or forex markets) where foreign currencies are bought and sold.

As a rough guideline, short-term means up to one year or possibly two years, and medium-term means two years to about five years, and long-term means over five years. Long-term capital also includes permanent finance such as equity shares and perpetual bonds.

The distinction between long-term and short-term, and between capital and money markets, is not always clear-cut. For example, commercial paper (CP) is a financial instrument used by companies to borrow money short-term typically for several months, but CP is issued within the framework of a long-term program in which CP is continually issued and repaid, according to the borrower's requirements. Because there is a cycle of issues and repayments within a single program, commercial paper can be described as both a money-market instrument and also as a means of raising long-term finance at a variable rate of interest.

Repo transactions also are related to both the money and capital markets. A repo transaction, or sale and repurchase transaction, involves a simultaneous arrangement to sell a quantity of high-quality bonds and to buy them back again at a later date, often the following day or just a few days later. In effect, although repo transactions involve the sale and purchase of bonds that are capital market instruments, they are secured short-term loans.

Cash Markets and Derivatives Markets

Financial markets are either cash markets or derivatives markets. In a cash market, investments, debts and money, for example shares, bonds, loans and deposits, are traded for immediate or spot delivery. The term derivatives markets are for financial instruments that have evolved or derived from cash-market instruments, but do not represent money or capital. Derivative instruments include options, futures and swaps.

Capital Market Instruments

A feature of most of the capital markets is that they trade in financial instruments. These

- are negotiable securities, i.e. they can be re-sold in a secondary market after they have been issued, and
- have long maturities, i.e. a long term to their eventual redemption and repayment, or are permanent and non-

redeemable or non-repayable, except at the option of the issuer, e.g. equity shares.

Capital market instruments can be grouped into several categories:

- equity instruments
- preference shares
- debt instruments, known as bonds
- hybrid instruments that combine elements of both equity and debt capital
- derivatives that are not used to raise long-term capital but are used by borrowers and investors to manage the cost or structure of their funding or investment portfolio.

The structure of the financial markets may be depicted as follows:

FINANCIAL MARKETS

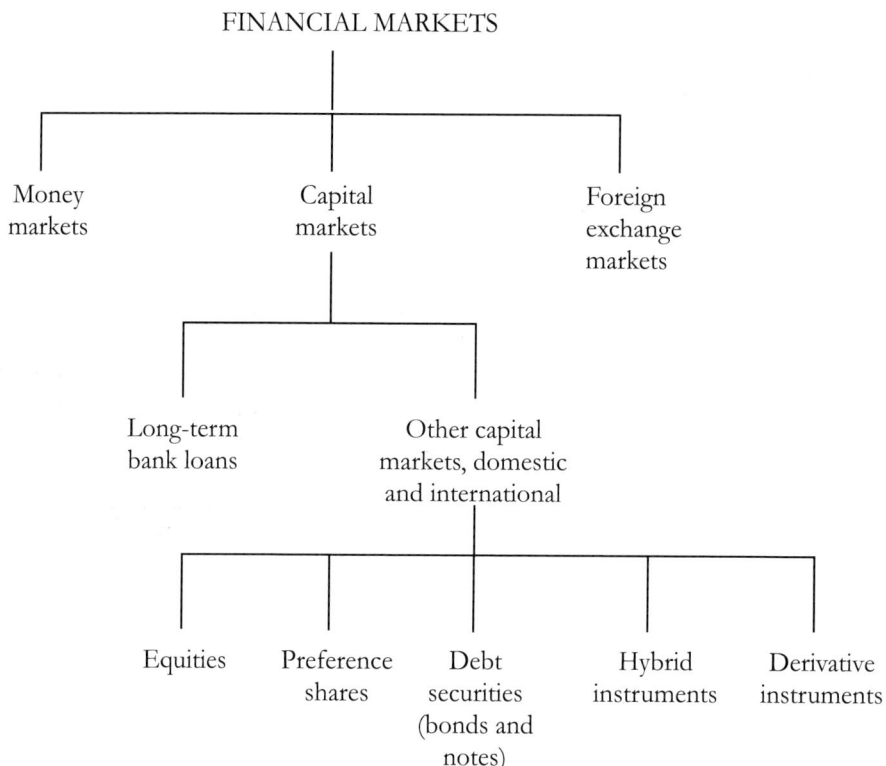

Domestic and International Markets

A distinction can be made between domestic and international capital markets.

Domestic Markets

A domestic market is a national market, created initially to meet the capital funding requirements of organizations within the country. A domestic market is subject to national laws, and is subject to regulation by one or more supervisory and regulatory bodies within the country. Before the capital markets became global, most investors and the intermediaries (brokers and dealers) in a domestic market were nationals. Despite globalization, the domestic capital markets are still essential for most small companies wishing to raise long-term capital through share issues or by means of bank loans.

As capital markets developed, many domestic markets opened up to both foreign investors and to foreign companies and other organizations wishing to raise finance. The US domestic equity and bond markets, for example, are significant sources of funding for many large international companies. Many intermediaries in the domestic markets, particularly investment banks, are now also international organizations, although usually with a local office in the domestic market's financial center. Some domestic markets, particularly those in countries with an advanced economy, have been successful in attracting international borrowers and investors. Domestic markets in less-developed and emerging economies have more difficulty in attracting international participation.

Occasionally, investors can buy shares or bonds of a foreign company in their own domestic capital market. In the US for example, investors can buy shares in some foreign companies in dollars in the form of American Depository Receipts or ADRs. Some international companies obtain a listing for their shares in several countries, and arrange for the shares to be traded on the major stock exchanges of those countries. A large European company, for example, might have its shares traded on the New York, London, Frankfurt and Paris stock exchanges.

National capital markets often are regarded as inadequate for meeting the requirements of international companies and investors, and there have been some developments towards the integration of domestic markets. The stock exchanges of Paris, Brussels and Amsterdam have merged to create the Euronext stock exchange, and during 2000 there was an unsuccessful proposal to merge the London Stock Exchange with the Deutsche Börse in Germany.

International Markets

An international capital market, as its name suggests, is one that operates internationally. Investors are located in different countries, and the organizations wishing to raise capital in the markets can be from any country, or are themselves international. More significantly perhaps, the intermediaries who operate the markets, advising organizations on share issues and bond issues, selling new issues of shares or bonds to investors, and operating a secondary market in securities, also are located in several countries. International markets may have major dealing centers, for example, London is a major center for the international capital markets, but their operations are not confined to those centers.

Participants in the international capital markets are subject to the national laws and regulations of the country in which they are located, but the market as a whole is outside the regulation of any individual national or supranational government body, and is self-regulating. Self-regulation is an essential ingredient of a successful international market, to enable the market to operate efficiently. For example, suppose that a French company wished to raise capital by issuing bonds, and selling some of the bonds to investors in the US, Germany, the UK and Japan. A system would be needed for selling the bonds internationally, providing for the delivery of the bonds to the investor and payment for the bonds by the investor, for holding the bonds (custody of the bonds), for providing information to market participants about prices and transactions, and for the resolution of any legal or other disputes.

In Europe, the international securities market has a self-regulatory code, and the market is organized by the International Securities Market

Association (ISMA), whose members consist of the main intermediaries in the market.

Unlike the domestic capital markets, the international capital markets are not open to small borrowers and investors. They are used for raising capital by governments, supranational organizations such as the World Bank, government organizations, banks and large non-bank companies. Medium-sized companies occasionally are able to issue bonds in the international market, but the market for high-yield bonds in Europe is not well-developed and is still very small.

A feature of the international markets is that companies issuing shares or bonds internationally often will arrange for the shares or bonds to be listed in at least one country. A company issuing bonds in Europe, for example, may arrange for the bonds to be listed in the UK, and accepted for trading by the London Stock Exchange. The bonds then will be traded internationally, either over-the-counter by telephone or by means of an electronic trading system. The process of obtaining a national listing, however, gives notice to investors that suitable checks have been made and procedures have been carried out to ensure the quality of the securities as investments.

The domestic and international markets operate in tandem. Investors wishing to invest in shares, bonds or other securities of an international company, or a foreign company, might do so by buying the securities:

- in the domestic market of the country concerned
- in the international market, or
- possibly in the domestic market in the investor's own country.

Domestic and International Capital Markets

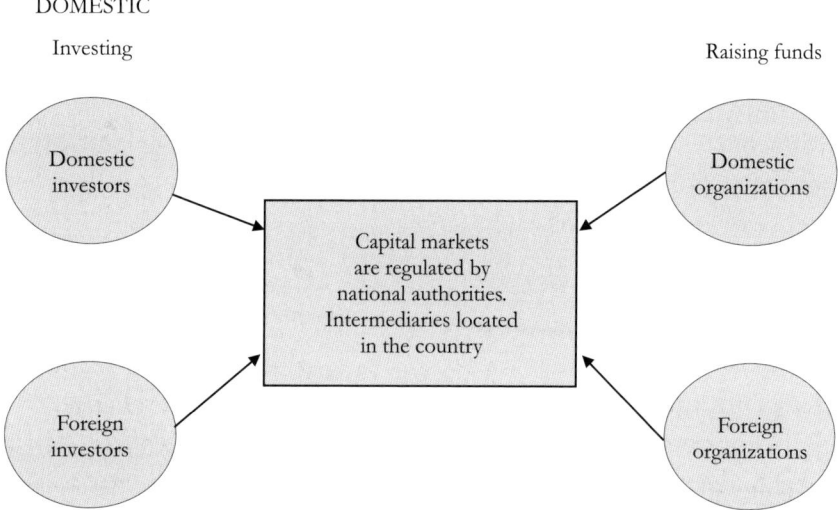

DOMESTIC

Investing

Raising funds

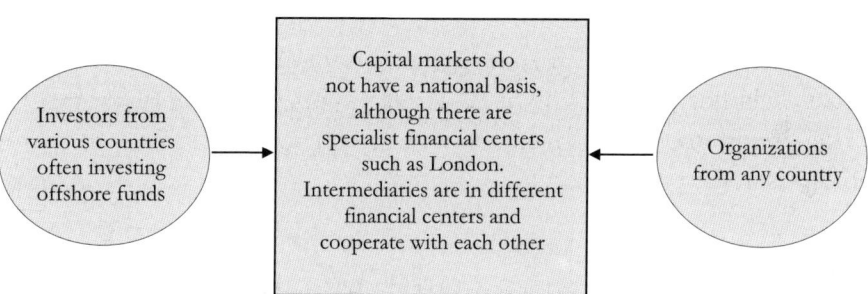

INTERNATIONAL

Primary and Secondary Capital Markets

A primary capital market is one in which organizations issue new securities, such as shares and bonds, in order to raise capital funding from investors. Investors buy the securities, providing money to the issuer in return for expectations or promises of future returns, in the form of dividends or interest.

A secondary capital market is not for raising capital. It is a market for buying and selling securities that have been issued already, and the securities are traded secondhand between investors. Secondary markets are important, however, because they give investors a means of cashing in their investment at a time of their choosing. The ability to sell investments readily adds to their value, and makes them more attractive to investors. For this reason, a successful primary market depends on the existence of a liquid secondary market.

The function of a stock exchange is to provide a secondary market for securities. A company wishing to issue shares, for example, will apply to the national listing authority for the shares to be listed, and to a stock exchange for the shares to be accepted for trading on the exchange. In the UK, for example, a company would apply for a listing to the UK Listing Authority that is part of the Financial Services Authority, and to the London Stock Exchange for admission of the shares to trading. Admission of shares to trading on the main London Stock Exchange is conditional on the shares being listed. The company then will issue the shares in the primary market, and the shares will be available immediately for trading in the secondary market.

In the international bond market, investment banks that arrange primary issues of bonds usually also will undertake to operate a secondary market in the bonds, in order to give the bonds greater appeal to potential investors in the primary issue.

Market Locations and Electronic Trading Systems

Some stock markets have a physical location where trading takes place on the floor of the exchange. Floor trading is now much less common that several years ago, but it still takes place in a number of exchanges, such as the New York Stock Exchange, Tokyo Stock Exchange and Chicago Mercantile Exchange. Orders to buy or sell securities are transmitted to dealers on the floor of the exchange, and the dealers then make the transaction.

In some stock markets, there is a centrally located regulatory body, and most brokers and dealers have offices nearby in the financial center, but there is no floor trading on the exchange. Examples are the London Stock Exchange and London International Financial Futures and Options Exchange (LIFFE). Other exchanges, such as NASDAQ, do not have a readily identifiable central location.

When trading does not take place between dealers on the floor of the exchange, transactions are made either by telephone or through an electronic dealing system. Dealing by telephone, referred to as over-the-counter dealing, is still common in most stock markets, but electronic trading systems are being introduced. It is now quite common for trading in securities in a market to be partly by telephone and partly electronically, for example on the London Stock Exchange and in the international securities market where ISMA has developed Coredeal, its own electronic exchange.

Market Participants

The participants in a capital market can be grouped into four categories: organizations seeking to raise capital by issuing securities (the issuers), investors, intermediaries and market regulators.

Intermediaries perform a number of different functions.

- Investment banks, securities houses and some other organizations advise companies and other organizations on primary market issues, and will arrange the issue, and either sell the securities to investors or underwrite the issue, that is undertake to buy up any shares or bonds that other investors will not buy at the offer price.
- Various organizations act as brokers, market makers or broker dealers in the secondary markets. Organizations operating in the primary market usually also will operate in the secondary market for the securities.

- Stock exchanges provide a forum and trading system within which trading in securities can take place. A stock exchange also has a regulatory function to ensure that trading in securities is conducted properly.
- Some intermediaries provide a system for the settlement of transactions in securities, whereby transactions are confirmed, and the securities are delivered to the buyer in exchange for payment. These intermediaries are either a clearing house operating on behalf of an exchange, or a central securities depository, such as Crest in the UK, and Euroclear and Clearstream, the European international CSDs. A central securities depository also provides investors with a system for holding securities in book-entry form, as a computer record rather than in the form of a share or bond certificate.
- Some organizations provide a custody service and hold securities on behalf of investor clients. They also carry out the administrative tasks related to the securities, such as ensuring that interest and dividend payments are received.

Intermediaries and Disintermediation

Disintermediation is a term that refers to the role of a securities house or investment bank as intermediaries in the primary capital markets. Securities houses and investment banks bring issuers of securities together with investors, but act only as a go-between. Unless they deal on their own account, investment banks do not provide capital to companies and other organizations.

This function differs from the role of lending banks that are mainly commercial banks, in the loans and deposits market. Banks take deposits from customers, and pay the customer interest, and they use the deposits to make loans to borrowers. A borrower raises capital from the bank, and has its transaction with the bank. The bank therefore stands between the investor (depositor) and the raiser of capital.

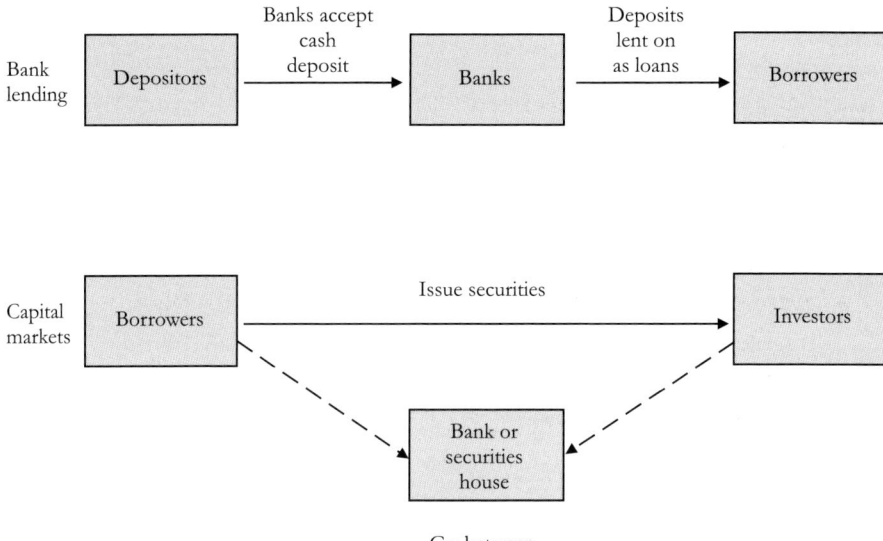

Go-between

Desirable Qualities of a Capital Market

A capital market should meet the needs of its participants, and in particular the needs of issuers and investors.

Issuers need to raise capital without difficulty, at a reasonable price or cost, and reasonably quickly.

Investors want to put money into securities that offer a good return, in the form of interest or dividends, and possibly also capital growth. Therefore they need a reasonable selection of securities in which to invest. They need also to be able to sell their investments easily, whenever they wish to do so, at a fair price.

The needs of issuers and investors are met by an efficient stock market, properly regulated. Efficient means a market in which information is readily available to investors, and in which dealing systems and back-office systems for settlement and holding securities function well and without error. A market also should be liquid, meaning that there must be ready buyers and sellers always available for securities, at a fair price.

Risk Management and the Capital Markets

Issuers and investors need to consider the financial risks associated with involvement in the capital markets.

Issuers should seek to:

- obtain the best price possible for the securities they issue
- avoid excessive borrowing, to the point where they might be unable to service their debts
- ensure, if possible, that they will be able to go back to the capital markets at any time to raise further long-term finance.

For investors, the chief risks are:

- Price risk. This is the risk that their investment will fall in value, probably because the actual returns are lower than the market was expecting. If a company declares lower profits and dividends than forecast, the value of its equity shares are likely to fall. If market rates of interest go up, the market value of its bonds are likely to fall.
- Credit risk. This is the risk that someone will fail to pay what is owed. In the context of investing in the capital markets, it refers largely to the risk that a borrower will fail to meet its obligations to pay interest or repay debt principal on schedule.
- Liquidity risk. In the context of investing in shares, bonds and other securities, it is the risk that the investor will be unable to sell its investments easily at a fair price whenever it wants to do so.
- Currency risk. This is the risk, in the context of investment, that an investor will buy securities denominated in a currency that subsequently falls in value against other securities. The fall in value of a currency can reduce, or even wipe out, the returns made on the securities.
- Counterparty risk. In some transactions, there may be a risk that the other party to a transaction will fail to carry out its side of the deal. For example, if one person sells shares to another,

counterparty risk is the risk that the seller will fail to deliver the securities for sale, as promised, or the buyer will fail to pay for them.

The most significant investors are institutional investors, such as pension funds and life assurance companies. A risk for them is that the returns they make on their investments are lower than the returns made by similar rival investors. Institutional investors therefore often compare the returns on their investments against some form of benchmark, such as the performance of a stock market index.

Capital Market
Instruments

Five broad categories of financial instrument are used in the capital markets: equity, preferred stock, bonds and other debt securities, hybrid instruments and derivatives. In addition, bank loans are a form of capital debt to many companies.

Equity and preferred stock, bonds and other debt securities, and long-term bank loans are all issued to raise funds. Derivatives, in contrast, are used to improve the management of capital rather than to raise new capital.

Securities

Securities is a general term used to mean financial instruments in the form of either a certificate or an electronic record, representing the ownership of a negotiable financial asset, such as shares, bonds or warrants.

Equity

An equity security is a share in a company that gives its owner a stake in the ownership of the company. The term equity is also applied to instruments such as options and warrants, and convertible bonds and preferred stock, that give their owner either the right to subscribe for equity shares, or the right to convert other securities into equity shares. In the US, equity is referred to as common stock and in the UK as ordinary shares.

When a company issues equity shares, it is selling part-ownership. The buyer or holder of equity shares is entitled to certain rights and liabilities, as part-owner of the company.

Equity shares normally carry three entitlements:

- to a dividend, payable out of the profits of the company
- to vote on resolutions at general meetings of the company
- to receive part of the capital of the company in the event of the company going into liquidation. Equity shareholders are entitled to a payment on liquidation only after the creditors of the company, including holders of debt securities, have been paid in full.

Equity shares have a nominal value, but usually are issued at a price in excess of this value. For example, the nominal value of shares in UK companies might be tycially any round amount up to $1, such as 5¢, 10¢, 50¢ or $1. All equity shares in a company in the same class have the same nominal value. The purpose of giving shares a nominal value is to provide a basis for payment of dividends. For example, succose that a company issues 20 million shares with a nominal value of $1 at a price of 300¢, and later issues a further five million $1 shares at a price of 450¢. Although the shares have been issued at different times and at different prices, every $1 share gives its owner the same entitlement as the owner of every other $1 share, regardless of the actual sale price at which the shares were issued.

Equity shares are permanent capital of the company. The shareholders cannot require the company to buy them back, and they remain in issue unless the company offers to buy them back and the shareholders accept the offer.

The return on investment for equity shareholders consists of a stream of dividends, payable out of distributable profits. The value of shares is a reflection of investor expectations of future dividends. Equity share prices therefore depend on market assessments of both the future profitability of a company, and possibly also the dividend policy of its directors.

If equity shares are traded in a secondary market, shareholders also can realize a capital gain or loss by selling them in the market at a price above or below the price at which they bought them.

Equity investors are the ultimate risk-takers in a company. If the company goes into liquidation, equity shareholders are not entitled to any repayment of capital until all other creditors and prior claims, e.g. preferred stockholders, have been paid off in full. Equity shareholders are not entitled to dividends unless all prior claims of other investors, bondholders and preferred stockholders have been met, and even then, the payment of dividends is at the discretion of the company's directors. As the ultimate risk-takers, equity shareholders are also the investors who benefit from growth in the company's profits. Rising profits will not affect the entitlements to interest or dividends of bondholders, lenders and preferred stockholders, but will increase the distributable profits available for paying dividends to ordinary shareholders. Equity shareholders therefore are the main beneficiaries of any growth in the company's profitability, and returns on equity are expected, in the long run, to exceed returns on any other form of financial investment.

Registered Shares and Bearer Shares
Shares are issued in either bearer form or registered form.

At one time, shares were issued in the form of paper certificates.

- Possession of the share certificate of bearer shares is evidence of ownership. The holder of a bearer share certificate is entitled to sell the shares and to receive dividends. A bearer share certificate is issued in the form of a paper certificate showing entitlement to a stated quantity of shares, for example, to shares to the nominal value of $10,000. Attached to the shares are dividend coupons, each individually numbered. When the company pays a dividend, it will pay the money on presentation of the appropriate dividend coupon, i.e. the coupon with the appropriate number. A shareholder is required to present the dividend coupon to a paying agent of the company such as a specified bank that will make the required payment. Because ownership of the shares is evidenced by possession of the share certificate, the company does not know at any time who its shareholders are unless the shareholders make their identities known. In addition, physical safeguarding of share certificates is a major concern, and all large investors in bearer shares use the services of a custodian or central securities depository to look after their investments.

- The ownership of registered shares is recorded in a share register, maintained either by the company or by a registrar acting on its behalf. The company issues paper share certificates that are evidence of ownership, but, unlike bearer shares, do not represent legal ownership. The record in the share register represents the legal ownership, and dividends are paid to the registered owner at the owner's registered address. When shares are sold, the legal title to the shares is not transferred until the change of ownership has been recorded in the share register.

Although the traditional form of shares is a paper certificate, major investors, and many private individuals, now hold their shares in electronic form, without any paper certificate. Shares in electronic form are described in several ways, such as shares in dematerialized form, in book-entry form, or as uncertificated securities. Shares are kept in a computerized share account by a centralized securities depository, recognized by both the relevant stock market and by the issuer of the shares.

Although shares can be held in electronic form, the concepts of bearer shares and registered shares continue. For example, ownership of bearer shares can be recorded electronically in systems such as those operated by Clearstream and Euroclear, but there is an underlying paper document representing the ownership of the shares that is held in safekeeping by a depository bank.

Registered shares are the norm in the US and the UK, but bearer shares are more common on the continent of Europe. Bonds also are issued in bearer or registered form, and most bonds issued in Europe are in bearer form.

American Depository Receipts (ADRs)

It is difficult, for legal and tax reasons, for investors in the US to hold shares in foreign companies. In addition, a US investor wanting to buy shares directly in a UK company would have to pay for them in sterling, and a US investor wanting to buy shares directly in a German or French company would have to pay in euros.

Instead, US investors may be able to invest in shares of a foreign company by purchasing American Depository Receipts, or ADRs. These represent shares in the foreign company that are held on deposit by a depository bank in the US.

ADRs are created by a non-US company placing a quantity of its shares on deposit with a depository bank in the US. ADRs are issued, each backed by a number of the shares placed on deposit. Regardless of the currency of the company's shares, ADRs are denominated in dollars. They can be given a stock market listing in the US, and can be traded in the same way as US company shares. When the company pays a dividend, the dividend is paid to the depository bank, and holders of ADRs are paid the equivalent amount in dollars.

The attraction of ADRs to non-US companies is that they can open up the US domestic share market, and enable the company to raise equity capital in the US. The advantage for US investors is that ADRs provide a readily marketable dollar equity investment in foreign companies.

- Some US banks specialize in ADRs, Bank of New York for example.

- ADR prices are in dollars. Dividends are paid in dollars.

- ADRs can be converted back into ordinary shares, by selling the ADRs back to the depository bank, and the bank selling the shares back to the company.

- The depository bank, as the legal shareholder, will vote at meetings of shareholders of the company in accordance with the wishes of the ADR holders.

Preferred Stocks

Preferred stocks are non-equity shares that entitle their holders to participate in dividends up to a specified amount and no further. The amount of dividend is fixed at a specified coupon rate, and a dividend usually is paid twice each year. For example, for 5% preferred stocks of $1, the annual dividend would be 5¢ per share, payable in two six-monthly amounts of 2.5¢ each.

A preferred dividend is paid out of the company's distributable profits, and will not be paid if these are insufficient to cover the amount of dividend payable.

There are five types of preferred stock.

- *Cumulative.* If the company is unable to pay a dividend, the unpaid dividend is accumulated and will be paid once the company has earned sufficient profits. Arrears of unpaid preferred dividends must be paid before equity shareholders can become entitled to a dividend.
- *Noncumulative.* Any unpaid dividend is not accumulated, and is forgone if the company cannot pay it out of available profits.
- *Participating.* Preferred stockholders receive a basic dividend plus some right to participate with equity shareholders in surplus profits.
- *Redeemable.* The company has the right to redeem the shares at some future time. Alternatively, there may be a fixed date when the company must redeem the shares.
- *Convertible.* The shares can be converted at some future date, at the option of the shareholder, into a specified quantity of ordinary shares of the company.

21

Preferred stock can be a combination of these types, e.g. redeemable and cumulative.

If the company goes into liquidation, preferred stockholders' rights to repayment of their capital – the nominal value of their shares, and possibly to unpaid arrears of dividends – are similar to the rights of unpaid creditors. However, preferred stockholders rank behind creditors but ahead of equity shareholders in order of right to payment out of the proceeds from selling off the company's assets.

New issues of preferred stocks are very rare in the capital markets. Preferred stock issues are more common in private companies, particularly private companies in which there is a significant amount of venture-capital funding.

Debt Securities

Debt instruments are issued for a specific term, with a final maturity date, and entitle their owner to periodic interest payments at a specified rate. At maturity, the debt principal is repaid. For example, 8% Treasury Stock 2009 is government loan stock that entitles its holder to interest at 8% per annum and is redeemable in the year 2009. 7¾% Treasury Stock 2012-2015 is redeemable at some time between the years 2012 and 2015, but with the specific redemption date to be decided by the issuer, i.e. the government.

Debt securities commonly are described according to their maturity (term to redemption) on issue. Government debt securities in the US and UK issued with a maturity of 91 days (three months) are known as Treasury bills. Short-term corporate debt instruments may be issued in the form of commercial paper. Medium-term debt securities are called notes, and are issued with a maturity of two to seven years. Long-term debt securities are called bonds.

Bearer Bonds and Registered Bonds
Bonds, like shares, are issued in either registered or bearer form, and

either as a certificate or in electronic book entry form. Most international bonds issued in Europe, for example, are bearer bonds. UK government bonds (gilts) are issued as registered bonds.

The holder of a bearer bond in certificate form is required to surrender the certificate at redemption in order to receive the principal repayment from the bond issuer.

Issuer, Principal, Interest and Maturity

A bond certificate will show prominently the key information relating to the bond issue:

- the name of the issuer
- the total amount (nominal value) of the debt issue
- the amount of debt represented by the certificate, and the amount the issuer promises to repay at maturity
- the rate of interest payable on the bond (the coupon), and
- the redemption date, when the debt principal will be repaid.

Bonds are categorized according to the type of issuer. Government bonds are issued by national governments in their domestic bond market, and the bonds of well-established governments are considered risk-free in their domestic market. They are risk-free because the government can create more money if necessary to repay the debt, and should not need to default. Bonds issued by governments in international markets usually are issued in a foreign currency, and so are not risk-free. Like other international bonds, they are given credit ratings so that investors can assess the credit risk when investing in them.

Corporate bonds are issued by companies. The main markets for corporate bonds include the US domestic market and the international bond markets. The US bond market is more accessible than the international bond market to small companies. Bonds with a credit rating below investment grade, many of them issued by small companies, are known as junk bonds.

Bonds are issued by other organizations, such as municipal corporations, and there is an identifiable market in the US for municipal bonds.

Coupon and Interest Payment Dates

The rate of interest payable on bonds is expressed as a percentage of the principal amount, i.e. of the face value or par value of the debt instrument, and is called the *coupon*. For 5% loan stock, for example, the coupon is 5% of the face value of the stock, not 5% of the market value and not 5% of the bond's issue price that could be above or below par value. The name coupon originates from bearer debt instruments. These are issued with interest coupons attached, in a similar way to dividend coupons with bearer shares. The investor must detach a coupon at the end of each interest period and present it to the issuer for payment.

The coupon rate of interest can be either:

- fixed for the full period to maturity (fixed-rate debt), or
- variable according to movements in market rates of interest (floating-rate debt).

The interest rate for floating-rate debt is reset at regular intervals according to specified terms. For example, floating-rate dollar eurobonds might pay 50 basis points (0.50%) over the six-month dollar London Interbank Offered Rate (LIBOR), and the rate of interest will be reset every six months to 0.50% above the LIBOR rate as at a given reference date, e.g. as at the reset date.

Interest usually is paid either six-monthly or annually. For example, if a bond has a face value of $100, and the coupon rate is 6% per annum, payable six-monthly, the gross interest payable will be $3 (3% of $100) every six months for each $100 nominal value of bonds.

Similarly, suppose a debt issue pays a floating rate of 0.50% above six-month LIBOR. If six-month LIBOR at the reference date is 5.5% per annum, and interest is paid six-monthly, the interest payment for each $100 of debt (nominal value) will be $3 (6/12 of [5.50 + 0.50]% x $100).

Secured and Unsecured Bonds: Guaranteed Bonds

Debt is either secured or unsecured.

- Secured debt gives the investor the protection of a legal claim on stated assets of the issuer in the event of default on interest payments or principal repayment. The assets are provided as security, and in the event of default on payment of interest or principal by the issuer, the bondholders can take legal action to appoint a person to take charge of the secured assets. The assets then will be disposed of, and the proceeds used to pay the secured bondholders.
- The unsecured debt investor relies entirely on the promise to pay by the issuer or a third-party guarantor. In the event of default on payment of interest or principal by the issuer, the bondholders must seek payment of what they are owed as unsecured creditors.

A bond issuer might have an issue of unsecured bonds guaranteed by a third party. The guarantor undertakes to make a payment of interest or principal in the event of default by the bond issuer. A guarantee from a reliable third party reduces the credit risk for investors, and makes a bond issue more acceptable to investors. When a group of companies uses a special finance subsidiary to issue bonds, investors will expect the bonds to be guaranteed by the parent company of the group. A national government might guarantee an issue of bonds by a state-owned organization.

International bonds normally are unsecured. When bonds are unsecured, the credit risk for investors could be high so it is usual for bonds to be given a credit-rating by at least one specialist credit-rating agency, and commonly two. The most well-known credit rating agencies are Moody's, Standard & Poor's and Fitch IBCA. A high investment-grade rating would give investors comfort that the risk from investing in the bonds should be fairly low. The price at which bonds can be issued, and/or the coupon payable on a bond issue, will depend to a large extent on the credit rating given to the issue.

- If there are two simultaneous bond issues, both with a coupon of 5%, the bond with the highest credit rating will be issued at a higher price.
- If there are two simultaneous bond issues, both at the same issue price, the bond with the highest credit rating will pay the lower coupon to investors.

Governing Law

Debt instruments are issued subject to the laws of a particular country. Investors seeking redress would have to take legal action under the jurisdiction of that country.

In Europe, a large proportion of international bonds are issued subject to the governing laws of England and Wales.

Types of Debt Security

Bonds vary in their characteristics. Some of the more common variations from straight fixed-rate term bonds are as follows.

FRNs (Floating-Rate Notes)

These are variable-rate debt securities, normally unsecured, long-dated and issued in the form of bearer bonds.

Zero Coupon Bonds

These are bonds that pay no coupon rate of interest. They are issued at a deep discount to their nominal par value and redeemed at par. The investor receives no interest payments; however, there is an interest yield from the capital gain, i.e. from the difference between the issue price and the eventual redemption value.

For example, five-year zero coupon bonds issued at a price of 74.73, i.e.

74.73 per 100 nominal value, and redeemed at par would give an investor an effective annual yield of 6%. This is illustrated below.

Issue price	74.73
Year 1 interest (6%)	4.48
	79.21
Year 2 interest (6%)	4.75
	83.96
Year 3 interest (6%)	5.04
	89.00
Year 4 interest (6%)	5.34
	94.34
Year 5 interest (6%)	5.66
	100.00

If the rate of return required by investors were to remain unchanged at 6% throughout the term to maturity, the market value of these bonds would increase to 79.21 at the end of Year 1, and 83.96 at the end of Year 2, 89.00 at the end of Year 3, 94.34 at the end of Year 4 and its redemption value of 100 at redemption. The market value of bonds redeemable at par will get closer to par as the redemption date approaches.

Deep Discount Bonds
These are bonds issued at a price well below par value and redeemed at par, offering a zero coupon or a low coupon rate of interest. Zero coupon bonds are a type of deep discount bond. An example of deep discount bonds would be ten-year bonds issued with a coupon of 3%, when the current yield required by investors on similar ten-year bonds is 7%. The bonds would have to be issued at a price well below par value in order to attract investors.

Subordinated Loan Stock
This is unsecured loan stock. In the event of a liquidation of the company, subordinated loan stock holders rank behind other unsecured

creditors in entitlement to payment from the liquidation of the company's assets. A high interest rate usually is required to compensate the loan stock investors for the higher credit risk.

Hybrid Instruments

Hybrid instruments are financial instruments containing features of both equity and debt. Common types of hybrid instrument are:

- convertible bonds or preference shares, and
- bonds with equity warrants attached.

Convertibles

Convertible securities (bonds or preference shares) entitle their holders at some specified date or dates in the future to change the securities into ordinary stock of the issuer at a pre-fixed rate of conversion. Until converted, the interest or preference dividend is paid.

The coupon for convertibles will be lower than the coupon rate for comparable straight debt, i.e. straight debt issued at the same time, because investors will be willing to receive less interest in return for the option to convert into equity.

The rate of conversion from debt into equity, fixed at the time of the issue, will anticipate an increase in the share price up to the date that the conversion rights can be exercised. For example, if common stock in Alpha Inc has a market value of $5 when it makes an issue of convertible stock at par, the terms of conversion might be just 15 shares for every $100 of stock. The market value of these shares, at the time of issuing the convertible stock, would be just $75, $25 below the par value of the stock. For bondholders to want to convert their bonds into shares when the opportunity to convert arrives, the shares would have to be worth over $6.67 each ($100 ÷ 15 shares).

Loan Stock with Equity Warrants Attached

Loan stock can be issued with equity share warrants attached. A share warrant entitles the holder on or after a future date to subscribe for a quantity of new shares in the company, at a fixed price. This subscription price is fixed when the loan stock is issued. It will be above the current market price for equity shares, in anticipation of a rise in the market price above the subscription price before the warrants become exercisable.

For example, a company might issue 5% bonds with warrants attached, and for every $1,000 of bonds, the investor might receive warrants to subscribe for 40 shares in the company, on or after a specified future date, at a price of $15 per share. At the time of the bond issue, the share price of the company would be less than $15.

Share warrants can be detached from the loan stock, and traded separately on the stock market.

Equity Derivatives

Some equity-related derivative instruments can be used to either hedge an investor's portfolio risk, or to speculate and seek high returns from a relatively small investment.

Traded Equity Options
Some stock exchanges trade equity options. An equity option is an instrument giving its holder the right, but not the obligation, to either buy or sell a quantity of shares in a company, at a fixed price (the exercise price) either on a future date or at any time up to a future date.

- An option giving its holder the right to buy a quantity of a company's shares at a fixed price is called a call option.
- An option giving its holder the right to sell a quantity of a company's shares at a fixed price is called a put option.

The exchange on which equity options are traded will specify the exercise prices at which options can be bought and sold. The buyer of a call or put option pays a premium to the seller (the option writer). If the holder of an option exercises the right to buy or sell at the fixed price, the seller of the option would be required to fulfill the obligation to either buy or sell at that price. In practise, when options are exercised, settlement is by means of a cash payment by the option writer to the option seller for the difference between the fixed price in the option and the current market price of the shares.

Traded options can be used to hedge price risk in a share portfolio, or to speculate for profit on future share-price movements. For example, if a speculating investor expects the price of shares in ABC Corporation to rise, he/she might purchase call options in ABC Corporation shares. The investor does not have to buy the shares, and the investment is restricted to the premium paid for the option. If the share price rises above the exercise price, the investor will exercise the options at a profit. If the share price does not rise above the exercise price, the option will not be exercised, and the premium payable for the options will have been lost.

Options also can be used to protect the value of a portfolio of shares. For example, suppose that an investor has a large quantity of shares in XYZ Corporation in an investment portfolio. He/she does not want to sell the shares, but is concerned about the fall in value of the portfolio from any fall in the share price of XYZ. It could be decided to buy put options in XYZ Corporation shares, giving the option to sell XYZ shares at a fixed price. If XYZ shares do fall in price below the exercise price, he/she will sell the options. The profit made on options dealing will offset the fall in the value of XYZ shares. He/she will have held on to the XYZ shares for long-term investment, but offset the fall in their value by making a profit on the options.

Stock Index Options
Stock index options are similar to traded options, with the difference that they are options on all the shares that make up a stock market index, rather than shares in an individual company. A stock index option gives its holder the right, but not the obligation, to buy (call option) or sell (put option) a notional portfolio of shares at a price represented by a

stock index value. For example, a call option might give its holder the right to buy a notional portfolio of shares in the FTSE100 stock market index at an index price of 6400. Each point rise or fall in the FTSE 100 index has a specific value in terms of the share option. If the FTSE index were to rise above 6400 before the option's expiry, the holder of a call option at 6400 would exercise the option, and would receive cash in settlement based on the extent to which the index is higher than 6400 on the option exercise date.

Equity Futures

A future is a standardized, exchange-traded contract, traded on a futures and options exchange. The most common type of equity future is a contract based on a stock market index. Each futures contract represents a notional portfolio of shares that makes up the particular stock market index. Futures are bought and sold on the futures exchange, at an agreed index price, for delivery at a future date. Standard settlement dates on futures exchanges are in March, June, September or December.

For example, an investor might buy a quantity of June futures in the S&P 500 index at a price of 1400. If the contracts run to settlement, the investor either will receive or pay a quantity of money in settlement, depending on whether the index is above 1400, in which case the buyer of futures at 1400 makes a profit, or below 1400. Buyers and sellers of futures can close their positions before settlement date by making an opposite transaction. For example, the buyer of 10 June S&P 500 futures contracts at 1400 can close his/her position before settlement date in June by selling 10 June S&P futures. If he/she can sell 10 futures at a price above 1400, a profit will be made on closing the position. Selling at a price below 6400 will mean recording a loss on futures dealing. Each index point has a standard value, and the profit or loss to the investor is calculated as the gain or loss in index points multiplied by the standard value per index point and the number of futures contracts.

Stock index futures, like options, can be used for either speculative purposes or to hedge the price risk in a share portfolio.

Most equity futures are contracts in a stock market index. However, the LIFFE exchange has begun trading futures contracts in the shares of some individual international companies.

Bond Futures

Just as there are equity futures, there are also bond futures. Some futures and options exchanges trade standardized futures contracts in a notional quantity of government bonds. For example, the CBOT exchange in Chicago trades futures in notional Treasury bonds, and the Eurex exchange in Frankfurt trades futures contracts in notional German government bonds (Bunds). Investors can buy or sell bond futures, for either speculative purposes or as a means of hedging interest-rate risk/ price risk in their bond portfolios.

Swaps

A swap is an agreement between two parties, usually a bank specializing in swaps transactions and a client organization, to exchange a stream of payments over a specified term, usually two to ten years. The payments are based on a notional amount of principal. One party makes payments of interest on one basis, and the counterparty makes payments on a different basis.

Interest-Rate Coupon Swap
One type of swap is the interest-rate coupon swap. In this type of arrangement, one party make payments on a notional amount of principal at a fixed rate of interest for the full term of the swap, and the other party makes payments of interest at a floating rate that is adjusted each interest period. Interest periods typically are every six or twelve months.

For example, Alpha and Beta may arrange a five-year swap in which they agree to exchange payments every six months on notional interest of $25 million. Alpha might agree to pay a fixed rate of 5.25% and Beta might agree to pay interest at the six-month dollar LIBOR rate. Every six months, there will be an exchange of interest payments between Alpha and Beta.

There are various reasons why coupon swaps might be used. In the context of the debt and equity markets, coupon swaps can be used by a company to switch the nature of its borrowing from fixed-rate to floating-rate interest, or vice versa. For example, a company might want to raise fixed-rate debt, but because of its size, it might be unable to issue fixed-rate bonds in the international bond market. Instead, the company might be able to borrow from a bank long-term, at a variable rate of interest, and arrange a swap, in which it pays interest at a fixed rate and receives interest at a floating rate. The net effect will be to make the company a payer of interest at a fixed rate.

Example
Gamma plc, a UK company, wants to raise six-year funds at a fixed rate of interest, but is unable to issue bonds in the international market. It arranges a six-year variable-rate loan with its bank for £10 million, on which it pays interest at LIBOR plus 100 basis points (1%). It also arranges a six-year swap on notional principal of £10 million, whereby it receives interest at LIBOR and pays a fixed rate of 6%.

As a result of the loan and the swap, Gamma effectively will be paying interest at 7% fixed.

		%
Loan interest:	Pay	- (LIBOR + 1.0)
Swap	Receive	LIBOR
	Pay	- 6.0
Net effective interest		- 7.0

Coupon swaps can be used by both borrowers of capital and investors to manage the mix of their fixed-interest and floating-rate interest debts or investments.

Currency Swap

A currency swap is an agreement between two parties to exchange a stream of payments in one currency for a stream of payments in another currency. A currency swap could involve the following exchanges:

- an initial exchange of a principal sum in one currency for an equivalent principal sum in a second currency
- a regular exchange of interest payments, for example six-monthly, on the principal sums exchanged
- at the end of the term of the swap, a re-exchange of principal amounts, at the same exchange rate as the initial exchange at the start of the swap.

A currency swap can be used by bond issuers in the capital markets to issue bonds in one currency, and switch to a liability (making payments) in a second currency of their preference.

Example

An Italian company wants to raise €150 million in fixed-rate debt. However, an investment bank has informed it that a good opportunity exists at the moment to issue bonds in sterling. Consequently the company arranges a bond issue in sterling, and a currency swap.

The arrangements might be as follows.

- The company issues £100 million (nominal value) of seven-year 5% sterling bonds, at par.
- It arranges a seven-year swap whereby it agrees to exchange £100 million for €150 million (exchange rate £1 = €1.50), with interest payable at 6% on the euros and at 5% on the sterling.
- At the end of the swap term in seven years, there will be a re-exchange of £100 million for €150 million. The Italian company will use the sterling received to redeem the bonds.

Throughout the seven-year period, the liability of the Italian company effectively will be in euros, with a commitment to pay interest at 6% per annum on €150 million, and to repay principal of €150 million at the end of the seven years.

Illustrative Currency Swap

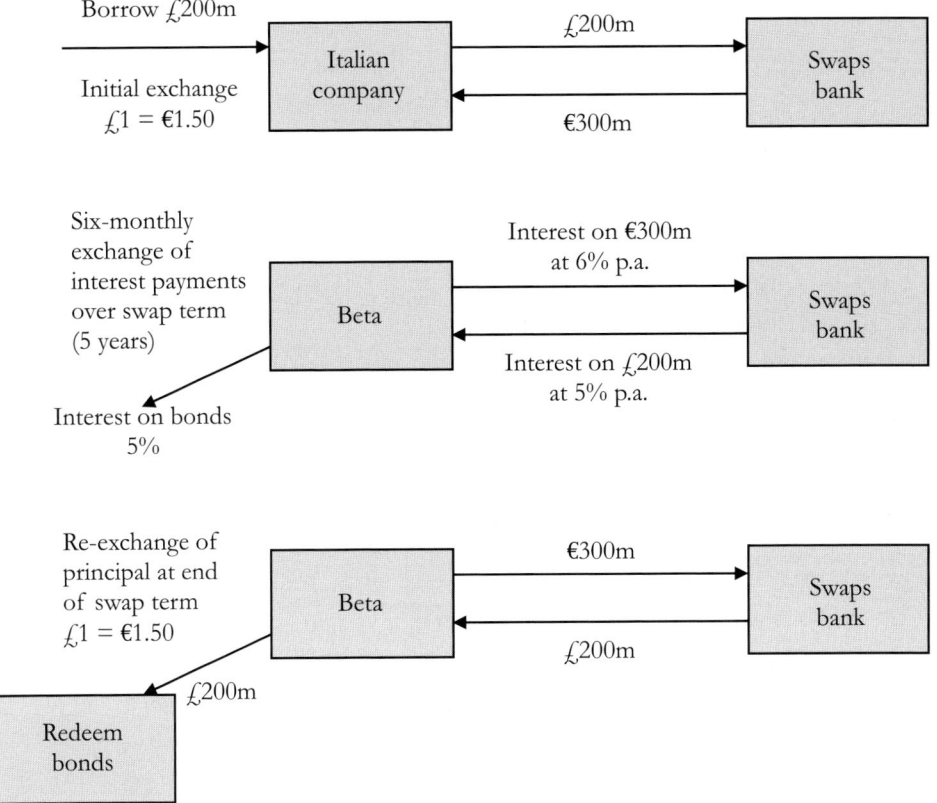

Market Participants

There are three main groups of participants in the capital markets:

- issuers
- investors, and
- intermediaries.

Markets also have regulatory bodies. There can be either self-regulation by an association or institute, direct government regulation, or a combination of government regulation and self-regulation. In the international capital markets, for example, participants are subject to the laws and regulations of the countries in which they operate, but there is also self-regulation by participants. Self-regulation in the international markets is concerned largely with ensuring that the markets operate efficiently across national borders.

Issuers

Issuers raise capital in the markets by making an issue of securities. They are mainly governments and government agencies, supranational organizations, banks and other companies.

Issuers seek to raise an amount of long-term funds, but there are several factors influencing how and when they do it.

- An issuer will want to have use of the funds for a certain period of time, perhaps permanently. The issuer therefore must decide the term to maturity of the issue, or choose between raising share capital or debt capital.

- An issuer of debt capital will want to raise capital at the lowest available cost, i.e. interest yield. The yield required by investors varies over time with changes in market rates of interest, and according to the term to maturity of the debt. The credit rating of the issue also can be significant. Investors will lend at a lower rate of interest to an organization with a high-grade credit rating because of the low credit risk.
- An issuer will seek flexibility to repay the capital obligation when it is in its best interests to do so.
- An issuer will look for funding company from sources that leave the opportunity to obtain further funding in the future, whether facilitating identical fungible issues or diversifying funding sources to allow access to other sources at a later date.

Governments and Government Agencies

A government may operate with a budget deficit. Meaning that its annual income from taxes and other sources is less than the amount that it spends. Budget deficits have to be financed. A central government can raise funds to finance a budget deficit by issuing debt capital. In the US, central government long-term debt instruments are called Treasuries, bonds or notes, according to their term to maturity on issue. In the UK, they are called gilt-edged securities or gilts. Governments also can borrow in the international capital markets by issuing sovereign bonds.

The amount and frequency of government borrowing depends mainly on the size of its budget deficit. The volume of public-sector borrowing sometimes can be so large that it dominates the domestic capital market for debt instruments. When this occurs, government bonds should be more attractive than the bonds of corporate issuers because the government should be a much lower credit risk than corporate borrowers. US and UK government bonds, for example, are considered virtually risk-free. To attract investors into their own bond issues when their government is borrowing heavily, companies must offer a higher coupon rate of interest than the current market yield on government bonds.

In recent times, some western governments, including those of the US and the UK, have been operating with a budget surplus that means they have been able to redeem bonds early, or have not had to issue new bonds to replace those that are maturing, i.e. have not had to refinance the debt. In contrast, the Japanese government has had a large budget deficit, and the market for Japanese government bonds (JGBs) is now very large.

Public-sector institutions and local-government authorities also can raise capital by borrowing in the markets. Their debt issues might be guaranteed formally or implicitly by the central government, and therefore should be a low credit risk.

Governments with a top-class credit rating usually can raise funds without much difficulty. However, when the amount of borrowing is large, it could be necessary to offer a higher yield, or to issue stock over a period of time, taking advantage of opportunities in the market when investor demand for government stock is strong. Even western governments are not assured of a top triple-A credit rating for their bond issues in the international bond markets.

Developing countries often are considered a high risk. In the Third-World debt crisis in the early 1980s, a number of developing countries defaulted on their bond issues. The governments of those countries are still able to raise funds in the international markets, but at a fairly high interest rate. A bond issue may be guaranteed by a supranational organization, such as the World Bank. In the US there are some dollar-denominated bond issues by developing countries known as Brady bonds. These are bonds for which the repayment of the debt principal at maturity, but not the payment of interest, are guaranteed by the US government.

Supranational Organizations
Supranational organizations are international bodies that use the capital markets to raise funds for re-investment, often in development projects. These include the World Bank, the Asian Development Bank and the

European Investment Bank. These organizations, supported by various national governments, have a high credit rating and are able to borrow in either the domestic capital markets of individual countries or in the international markets. The World Bank is one of the largest borrowers in the international bond markets.

Non-Bank Companies

Many non-bank companies rely mainly on retained profits and bank loans for long-term finance. However, they also tap the capital markets for new funds if they are able to do so.

When interest rates are low, large companies that are able to issue international bonds may try to raise all their new long-term capital in the form of bonds. Unlike dividend payments on shares, interest payments on debt are an allowable expense for tax purposes. The tax relief on debt interest can make debt finance much cheaper than equity finance.

Example

A company wants to raise $100 million in long-term capital. If it issued equity, shareholders would expect a return of 7% on their investment. Another option is to issue ten-year bonds with a 5% coupon. Taxation on corporate profits is at the rate of 30%.

Analysis

The cost of issuing equity would be 7%. Dividends on the new shares would have to be $70,000 each year, or if they were lower than this initially, the new shareholders would expect profits growth and dividend growth over time. The cost of issuing bonds would be fixed for the full ten-year period. If the rate of tax is unchanged, the effective cost of the bonds after tax would be 3.5%, which is 70% of 5%. The bonds would be much cheaper.

Companies are restricted from borrowing more than they do when interest rates are low by the demands of lenders and bond investors. High levels of debt increase the credit risk, i.e. the risk that the company may default on its debt payments. A condition of a bank loan or bond issue might be a requirement for the company to give a promise or covenant not to allow its total borrowing to exceed a certain amount. Failure to keep this promise would constitute an event of default, and give the lender or bond investors the right to demand immediate repayment of the debt.

Finance Subsidiaries

Some international companies use finance subsidiaries to raise funds for the rest of the group. A number of European companies, for example, have a finance subsidiary based in the Netherlands. The finance subsidiary arranges debt issues in its own name in order to raise debt capital for the operating companies in the group. European companies also might have a US finance subsidiary whose task is to raise funds for the company in the US markets.

Having obtained funds, the finance subsidiary will lend them to the group's operating divisions, usually at an arm's-length commercial rate of interest. Finance subsidiaries, by acting as a banker for the rest of the group, can provide the expertise for raising funds, for example in foreign markets, and can apply financial controls over the group's operating divisions more effectively than external lenders or investors.

Debt issues by finance subsidiaries probably will have to be guaranteed by the parent company.

Banks

Banks, like other companies, raise funds in the domestic and international capital markets. Because banks require large quantities of funds to sustain their lending business, they are relatively large issuers.

Many of the funds of commercial banks (lending banks) come from customer deposits, but a bank also must have an adequate amount of long-term capital, both equity and long-term debt, to protect their customers against the risk of lost deposits. The aim of the Basle Agreement, an international agreement on the capital adequacy of banks adopted by most countries, is to ensure that banks have a minimum amount of long-term capital relative to the size and risk of their business.

When banks make losses, their capital base shrinks. As a consequence, they must:

- reduce the volume of their lending activities, or
- lower the credit risk in their lending, and stop lending to risky customers, e.g. avoid company loans, or
- raise additional capital in the markets, by issuing equity or bonds.

Issuing fixed-rate bonds also gives banks a source of fixed-rate funding they can use to offer interest-rate coupon swaps to other companies seeking to swap from variable-rate to fixed-rate funding.

Asset-Backed Securities

For many bond issues, the identity of the issuer is important in persuading investors to buy the bonds. For asset-backed securities, the nature of the assets owned by the issuer, rather than the identity of the issuer, is the key consideration for investors.

Asset-backed securities are issued by specially established companies, sometimes called special-purpose vehicles or SPVs. An organization with a portfolio of assets that will earn a predictable stream of income into the long-term future, will sell these assets to an SPV. For example, a bank might have a portfolio of mortgage loans that it wishes to sell to an SPV, to raise immediate cash. The SPV will issue bonds, and pay for the interest-earning assets with the proceeds of the issue. Investors in the bonds issued by the SPV will receive a coupon rate of interest, but payment of the interest will be guaranteed by the interest received from the underlying assets that it now owns. The bonds of the SPV are backed by the interest-earning assets, and an investor in the bonds effectively is investing in the future income stream from those assets.

Asset-backed securities can be issued for any type of asset with a predictable long-term future stream of income. A bank can use them to sell off assets that it no longer wishes to hold, perhaps in order to comply with capital-adequacy regulations.

Deciding What to Issue

An issuer can raise funds by issuing equity, debt or hybrid instruments. In broad terms, concerns with an issue should be:

- to maintain a satisfactory level of financial gearing, and to avoid excessive financial risk from over-borrowing
- to select the currency in which to raise the capital
- to avoid, if possible, a dilution of earnings per share for equity shareholders
- to obtain shareholder consent for new issues of equity, particularly when the issue is not a rights issue and calls for some sacrifice of pre-emption rights
- to select the appropriate maturity of the issue
- to consider the tax rules and other regulations that apply to different types of capital in different countries, and arrange a capital issue that provides tax benefits to the issuer or investors
- to make sure that the issue is a success, which means it must appeal to targeted groups of investors.

Investors

The capital markets in most countries are dominated by institutional investors, both domestic and foreign. The main investing institutions vary from country to country, depending on the national financial framework. In general, however, they consist of:

- insurance and life assurance companies
- investment companies
- banks
- pension funds

- unit trusts/mutual funds.

These organizations obtain funds, in the form of life assurance premiums, pension contributions, and investments by retail investors, that they invest in a range of investments, mainly financial instruments. The task of making the investments and managing the investment portfolios is often assigned to specialist fund managers.

The purpose of investing is to earn a return or profit. This takes the form of interest or dividends, and perhaps also a capital gain from reselling an investment for more than its original purchase price.

The yield (or capital gain) that investors expect to receive in the future will be a major factor in their decisions to subscribe to an issue. However, the interest rate for a bond issue might on occasion have to be higher than the rate the issuer is willing to pay, and in this situation the issue would not take place perhaps until market interest rates come down.

Although a high return will be sought, there are other factors that will influence decisions about whether to invest in particular issues. These are:

- comparable yields
- investment risk, and
- liquidity in the secondary market

The expected yield on an investment should be comparable with the expected yield from similar securities in the market.

Investors must accept some risk of loss. The value of stocks and shares can fall below the issue price or purchase price, and investors would suffer a capital loss. There is also the risk that an issuer of debt capital will default on its obligations to pay interest or fail to repay the loan principal at maturity. Investment institutions either will refuse to invest in issues that they consider too risky, for example an issue that does not have an investment-grade credit rating, or will invest only if the expected return justifies the risk.

Investors often want the flexibility to switch funds from one investment to another and therefore will want the secondary market to be liquid for most of the securities in their portfolio. This creates a tendency to invest in well-established markets, and to avoid investing in securities that would be difficult to resell. In addition, institutional investors normally will be more willing to subscribe to new issues when they have a lot of cash on which to draw.

Market Sentiment

Capital markets can be driven by sentiment. The willingness of investors to subscribe to a new issue can be governed by the mood of the investment community at the time. When there are concerns about a slowdown in economic growth and a decline in company profits, it will be very difficult for companies to raise new capital by issuing equity shares. In contrast, when prospects for rapid growth in company profits are high, investor demand for new equity is likely to be high.

A fairly recent example of this was the heavy demand during 1999 for shares in internet companies on the expectation of rapid growth in e-commerce. The internet bubble burst in 2000, and share prices in these companies fell dramatically followed by a number of widely reported insolvencies. After the share price collapse, it became extremely difficult, if not impossible, for internet companies to raise new capital.

Intermediaries: Investment Banks and Securities Houses

A number of crucial services are provided in the capital markets by investment banks and securities houses. They launch new issues on behalf of client companies (taking a fee for their services) and encourage investors to subscribe to the issue, perhaps by selling an issue to their existing client base of investment institutions.

Intermediaries in the capital markets do not invest their own money.

Their role is to match the issuers of securities with investors, and to advise the issuer on what financial instruments would be best suited to investors' needs of the moment.

The *timing* of issues can be important, and intermediaries must maintain regular contacts with clients in order to identify a window of opportunity for a new issue, whereby the interests of both the issuer and the investor can be satisfied. Without regular client contact, an intermediary cannot recognize opportunities that exist.

For example, if an intermediary is aware that several investment institutions are keen to buy a particular type of security yielding a given rate of interest, for example convertible bonds, or yen-denominated bonds, it can suggest to a client planning to raise capital at some time in the future that now might be a good time for an issue.

Intermediaries are more likely to attract investors if they agree to make a *secondary market* in the securities after issue, perhaps by providing two-way prices to investment clients. A market maker in securities must hold some of the stock on its own account, and this puts the intermediary's own capital at risk of losses if the market price falls. However, the advantages for an investment bank of market making, or dealing on its own account in the securities of client firms, are:

- the potential for trading profits from dealing in the securities, and
- enhanced placing power because more investors will be prepared to invest if there is a secondary market.

Other intermediaries deal in the secondary markets as brokers, on behalf of clients or on their own account.

Because of their specialist knowledge of the markets, intermediaries can give the best advice and service to corporate clients seeking to raise funds. The main banks active in the capital markets commonly are referred to as investment banks.

The term merchant bank was used at one time within the UK and some Commonwealth countries such as Australia and New Zealand, but the term investment bank is now predominant because the market is dominated by US banks. The term securities house is used more generally to refer to an organization that provides an intermediary role in the primary capital markets.

The large investment banks specialize in international as well as domestic capital markets, and act as lead manager in international equity and bond issues. To do this they must have a strong presence in the markets, with the placing power ability to find foreign investors to subscribe to an international issue. League tables are published regularly showing which intermediaries have placed the most new funds in particular markets.

The main activities of investment banks in the equity and bond markets are:

- origination
- syndication and underwriting
- distribution (selling an issue), and
- secondary market trading.

Origination

On the buy side, intermediaries must find clients who want to issue securities to raise funds. Major intermediaries will seek to build up a client portfolio, a list of clients who regularly tap the capital markets for funds. In the domestic equities market, listed companies seeking to issue new shares will go through a main sponsor or securities house. A new company coming to the market for the first time will approach a securities house that will decide whether or not to act as its sponsor.

In the international capital markets, intermediaries must often sell fund-raising ideas or opportunities to clients, and a large company might not use the same intermediary each time it makes an issue. The process of promoting an issue involves:

- finding clients who could be interested
- persuading the client
- negotiating the terms and conditions of the issue
- becoming the *lead manager* for the issue by preparing the

documentation for the issue, organizing the procedures for the issue on the client's behalf, and making arrangements for the sale of the issue to investors

- organizing the underwriting and the selling for the issue.

New Issues: Factors for the Investment Bank to Consider
There are several factors that an intermediary must consider for any planned new issue.

- Is the issuer creditworthy? The issue will be given a credit rating, and the rating it receives will affect the success of the issue, and the price at which the bonds can be issued.
- Is the issue attractive to investors? Is it an appropriate type of security, for which there is current investor demand? Is it correctly priced?
- Is the timing of the issue right?
- Will the fee be sufficient to justify the costs and efforts of the issue?
- Is the intermediary's relationship with the client a significant factor in the decisions about making the issue?

Underwriting
Having negotiated an agreement with a client for a new issue, the lead manager must deliver on the promise to raise funds. This can be done by putting together a group of financial institutions to underwrite the issue in return for a fee or commission.

Underwriters guarantee to take up any of the issue, at the issue price, that is not taken up by other investors. If the issue has been priced correctly, underwriters should not have to buy any of the issue that will be sold to other investors, and their fee will be pure profit.

In the international bond market, a bond issue is syndicated and the issue normally is underwritten by a group or syndicate of banks. In the US some syndicated issues are not underwritten. Instead, the syndicate banks agree to make their best efforts to sell the issue without committing themselves to buy any unsold stock.

Selling an Issue

An intermediary must sell an issue on the client's behalf, and will make a number of sales presentations to potential investors. In the domestic capital markets, the task of selling an issue rests mainly with the securities house that is acting as sponsor and main market maker. The securities house will try to place the issue in firm hands, i.e. with investors who are unlikely to try to resell their securities soon after the issue. Following a weak or loose placement, many investors will try to sell their securities at a profit soon after the issue, and the market price therefore is likely to slip and remain low for some time.

In the international capital markets, the task of *distribution* (selling the issue) normally will be taken on by all the banks in the syndicate assembled by the lead bank. One or more banks, possibly the lead bank, will be the book runner for the issue, monitoring the progress of the sales efforts by the banks in the selling syndicate..

Secondary Market Trading

Some intermediaries make a market for the secondary trading of selected securities. A secondary market might be operated through a stock exchange, with intermediaries acting as brokers, dealers or market makers in the market. Alternatively, a secondary market might be operated outside the framework of a stock exchange.

There are several ways of operating a secondary market in securities.

- On the New York Stock Exchange, the most liquid stock market in the world, trading in shares is by auction on the trading floor of the exchange, driven by supply and demand, and organized by a specialist for the securities.
- Some secondary markets operate through a central electronic order book, where buying and selling orders are input, matched and executed. Intermediary firms will maintain a secondary market by trading in securities on their own account, buying and selling in order to maintain a liquid market, and to make profits on their dealing activities.
- Some secondary markets operate with market makers. A market

maker undertakes to provide continuous price quotations to the market for the prices at which they will buy (bid price) and sell (ask price or offer price) quantities of the shares. Anyone wishing to buy or sell shares can transact a deal with the market maker offering the most favorable price. Intermediaries fulfill the role of market makers in selected stocks. Market makers try to create a liquid secondary market in which the spread between bid and offer prices can be narrow, and profits will accumulate through the large volumes of shares or bonds traded.

Role of investment banks in the equity and bond markets

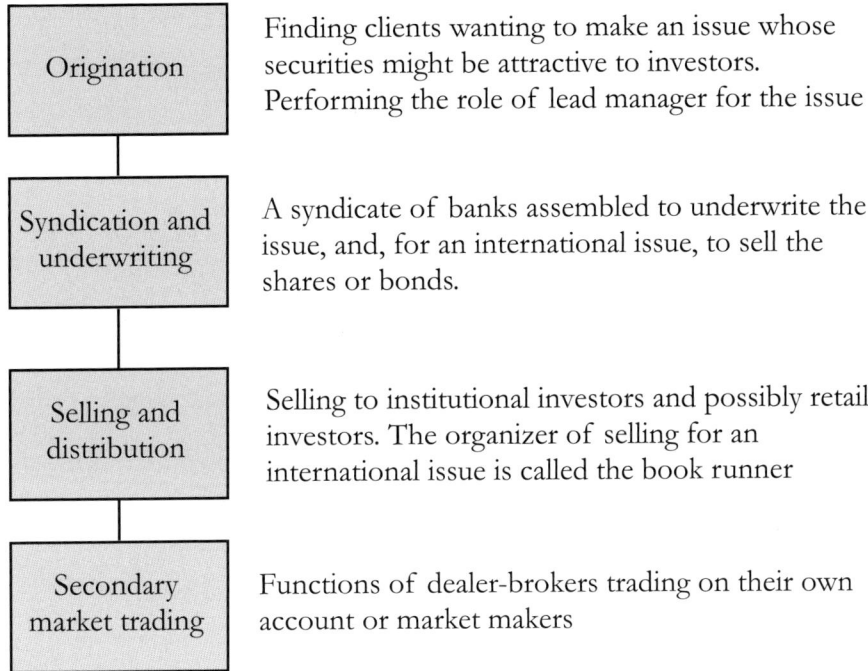

| Origination | Finding clients wanting to make an issue whose securities might be attractive to investors. Performing the role of lead manager for the issue |

| Syndication and underwriting | A syndicate of banks assembled to underwrite the issue, and, for an international issue, to sell the shares or bonds. |

| Selling and distribution | Selling to institutional investors and possibly retail investors. The organizer of selling for an international issue is called the book runner |

| Secondary market trading | Functions of dealer-brokers trading on their own account or market makers |

Brokers

A buyer or seller of securities can deal with a market maker either directly or through a broker. A broker is an intermediary who acts on behalf of clients wishing to deal in securities. A broker does not quote prices, but obtains a price for a client from a market maker, and then executes transactions as instructed by the client, and charges a commission for the service.

Inter-dealer brokers (IDBs) act as intermediaries for trades between market makers. A market maker or broker-dealer who is short in an item of stock might have to buy from another market maker or dealer, but will want to keep secret its identity as a buyer of the stock. Using an IDB for the transaction provides the anonymity. There are specialist IDBs, for example, in the UK gilts market. Another way of maintaining anonymity as a buyer or seller in the market might be to trade through an electronic trading system, such as an Electronic Communications Network (ECN) within the Nasdaq stock market.

Central Securities Depositories

A central securities depository (or CSD) is an organization that provides a means whereby members or client firms can hold securities in electronic form. There are CSDs in various countries, such as the Depository Trust Company, part of the Depository Trust and Clearing Corporation or DTCC in the US, and Crest in the UK. In Europe, there are two large international CSDs, Clearstream and Euroclear, that provide a system for holding both international and some domestic securities in book-entry form.

CSDs maintain electronic stock accounts for their members, but also arrange for payment instructions to be sent to a buyer's settlement bank, and for transfers of payments to be made from the buyer's bank to the seller's bank at settlement. All members of Crest, for example, are required to nominate a settlement bank that must have a computer link to the Crest system.

Clearing, Settlement and Netting of Transactions
Transactions in equities and bonds have to be settled. Settlement involves payment for the securities by the buyer and delivery of the

securities to the buyer by the seller. Ideally, payment and delivery should happen at the same time so that there is delivery versus payment.

Before a transaction can be settled, certain back-office procedures must be performed. These include:

- matching and confirming the transaction. The buyer and seller should check the details of the transaction they think they have made. Any misunderstandings and disagreements must be identified and rectified
- sending instructions for payment for securities or delivery of securities to the appropriate organization or individual.

As stated above, organizing the settlement of transactions may be the responsibility of a national or international CSD.

In some exchanges, the exchange, or more accurately, an organization acting on behalf of the exchange, will guarantee the performance of the transaction to both the buyer and the seller. Although the buyer and seller make the transaction, the exchange steps in between them, and acts as the seller in the transaction for the buyer, and as the buyer in the transaction for the seller. In this way, the exchange gives its guarantee to both the buyer and the seller that the transaction will be honored, and there is no counterparty risk, i.e. risk that the other party to the transaction might fail to carry out their side of the deal.

This intermediary role is performed by a number of specialist organizations, either for one exchange or for a number of different exchanges. In the US the role is performed for transactions in most equities and corporate bonds by the National Securities Clearing Corporation (NSCC), a part of the DTCC. In the UK the London Clearing House performs this service for the LIFFE futures and options exchange and the Tradepoint stock exchange, and has discussed performing a similar role for the London Stock Exchange.

When the exchange guarantees transactions by acting as counterparty to all buy transactions and all sell transactions on an exchange, the organization performing the role of intermediary can provide a netting service to its users. A firm of brokers may carry out a large number of transactions on a stock exchange on any one trading day. If all these transactions are with the exchange or its representative organization, the broker may be required to settle all the transactions on any one day by making a single net payment to the exchange, or by receiving a single net payment from the exchange. There is no need to settle every transaction individually.

A netting service is provided, for example by the NSCC in the US, for almost all transactions in shares and corporate bonds on any exchange in the US. This improves the efficiency and reduces the cost of settlement.

Regulators

Domestic capital markets are regulated by institutions and national laws of the country in which they operate. Laws and regulations vary between countries, but the primary aim of any market regulation should be to protect investors by ensuring an orderly market with fair working procedures. There has been a trend towards greater market regulation. For example, in the UK additional regulatory powers have been given to the Financial Services Authority, a government agency, by the Financial Services and Markets Act 2000.

Users of international capital markets are subject to the regulations of the countries in which they operate. They also are expected to comply with the voluntary codes of the market, including self-regulatory codes and guidelines issued by a body representing market intermediaries, such as ISMA in the international capital markets.

4

The Markets

The world's capital markets have evolved, and continue to evolve, to satisfy the needs of issuers, investors and intermediaries.

- Regular issuers of equities or bonds need ready access to long-term funds at a reasonable price. International companies are prepared to offer their securities to investors in many countries.
- Investors look for a satisfactory return for a given investment risk, and want the expectation of higher returns to justify higher investment risk. They also prefer markets to be liquid, to give them the flexibility to switch their investments. As a general rule, investors also prefer the protection of a formal, regulated market.
- Intermediaries seek to encourage market activity, and often try to encourage initiatives that might increase the volume of transactions in securities.

Issuers, investors and intermediaries have several interests in common, including:

- improved structures and systems for issuing and trading securities internationally
- more efficient trading systems
- more efficient back-office systems for clearing and settlement of transactions.

The Evolution of Domestic and International Stock Markets

Domestic stock markets were developed to satisfy the needs of domestic companies and the domestic government for capital. Investors principally were domestic institutions and individuals. Over time, however, most domestic stock markets have become, to a greater or lesser degree, more international.

- Foreign investors may buy shares and bonds in the domestic markets of other countries. Large institutional investors have investment portfolios in a number of currencies. Some investment funds even specialize in foreign investments.
- Issuers may be able to sell their shares or bonds in the domestic market to foreign investors. US companies issuing bonds or shares in the US, for example, are likely to attract interest from European and Asian investors.
- Foreign companies may issue shares or bonds in the domestic market of another country. A UK company, for example, may make a bond issue in the US in order to attract the interest of US investors who would be less interested in an international bond issue in Europe.
- Stock markets provide for trading in shares of foreign companies, including shares that already are traded on one or more stock markets in other countries.

The increasing globalization of capital market issues and of the investment community, have led to speculation that most domestic stock markets are too small and inefficient, and that stock exchanges have to become more international. In 2000, the Paris, Amsterdam and Brussels stock markets merged to form Euronext, a single exchange. Further mergers of domestic stock markets should be expected.

Overseas Listings
Some large international companies choose to have their shares traded on several domestic stock markets around the world. Shares that are traded on a stock market in a foreign country are sometimes called overseas listings. Large non-US companies, for example, might seek a listing on the New York Stock Exchange:

- to broaden the share ownership, to include more US investors
- to provide a liquid secondary market in the shares for US investors, and
- to improve the visibility of the company, perhaps as a prelude to expanding their operations in the US.

Similarly, a number of non-UK companies have their shares traded on the London Stock Exchange, for similar reasons. LIFFE, the London-based futures exchange, trades futures in the shares of a small number of US and European companies.

Development of the International Markets

The international capital markets have evolved in response to the desire of issuers to seek a wider investor base, and of investors to build up a more international investment portfolio. The growth of the international markets has been assisted by improvements in communications and technology, as well as the growing international presence of the major investment banks.

Oddly perhaps, it is quite common for shares or bonds that are issued and traded in the international markets to be listed in at least one country, and for the securities to be admitted for trading on a major stock exchange in that country.

- An international bond issue in Europe, for example, might be listed in the UK and admitted to trading on the London Stock Exchange, even though the shares are issued by selling them through an international banking syndicate and secondary market trading is conducted through the international market, in accordance with ISMA rules and guidelines.
- When a company makes an international issue of equity, the shares will be expected to rank equally with all other equity shares of the company. This means that the shares must be listed in the same country as the company's other shares, and admitted to trading on the same stock market or markets.

Secondary Market Trading: Order-Driven and Quote-Driven Trading Systems

Shares and bonds can be traded in either of two-ways, within an order-driven system or within a quote-driven system.

Order-Driven Systems
In an order-driven system, trades in securities are driven by order to buy or to sell coming into the market. Buy orders are matched with sell orders, and transactions are made. A successful order-driven system depends on a large volume of buy and sell orders coming to the market, a liquid market, as well as an efficient method of matching orders.

The New York Stock Exchange has an order-driven system, whereby buy orders and sell orders come to the floor of the exchange, and transactions are made by supply and demand, in a form of auction system. On average, it takes less than 30 seconds from an order being submitted to the exchange to the order being fulfilled and conformation being sent back to the person sending in the order.

More commonly, order-driven systems are based on some form of electronic trading system or order book. Orders are input to the system, where they are matched and transacted. Orders that are not matched and transacted will drop out of the system without being executed. To ensure that the market is sufficiently liquid, some investment banks will operate as broker-dealers, making buy or sell transactions on their own account with orders input by others into the order book.

Quote-Driven Systems
In a quote-driven system, a number of market-makers undertake to provide continuous two-way prices in a share or bond. Two-way prices are a bid price, at which the market maker will buy the security, and an ask price or offer price, at which it will sell the security. Investors can then arrange transactions with market makers at the prices they are quoting. Market makers expect to make a profit from the difference

between the prices at which they buy and the prices at which they sell securities, and they will adjust their quoted prices in response to demand and supply in the market.

The prices of market makers are displayed on price-quotation screens, and so are continually accessible to institutional investors.

Floor Trading, Over-the-Counter Trading and Electronic Trading Systems

Secondary market trading in shares and bonds may be on the floor of the exchange, conducted over the counter or by an electronic trading system.

- Trading on the floor of a stock exchange is nowadays rare, particularly outside the US. However, floor trading still takes place at the New York Stock Exchange.
- Over the counter or OTC trading is a term used to describe trading by telephone. An investor wishing to buy or sell securities might check prices that are being quoted by market makers, telephone the market maker offering the best price, and transact the deal by telephone. The order then will be confirmed, possibly by an exchange of telex messages. Some OTC trading is still carried on, for example on the Nasdaq stock market and for shares in some companies on the London Stock Market. However, it is gradually being superseded by electronic trading systems that can be more efficient and cheaper.
- In an electronic trading system, orders to buy or sell securities together with details of the quantities to buy or sell, minimum or maximum acceptable price, and so on, are input to the system where they are matched with corresponding orders and automatically transacted. Electronic systems have been making rapid headway in recent years, and are used for example by the

Nasdaq stock market, the London Stock Exchange, the Frankfurt Stock Exchange and even the international stock market where ISMA has introduced the Coredeal trading system for its members.

The Stock Markets

Some stock markets are larger and much more developed than others. The major US stock markets are the New York Stock Exchange and the Nasdaq stock market, although there are other stock exchanges, such as the American Stock Exchange. Nasdaq and the American Stock Exchange are part of the same group. Within Europe, the major stock markets are London, Frankfurt and the Euronext exchange. Within Asia, the major stock market is in Tokyo.

New York Stock Exchange
The NYSE on Wall Street is still the largest stock exchange in the world, providing a market in US government securities (Treasuries) as well as corporate shares and bonds. Trading in shares is conducted on the floor of the exchange, but trading in Treasuries is over the counter. Although the NYSE is the largest stock exchange in the US, many companies list their shares on other exchanges, principally Nasdaq and the American Stock Exchange in New York.

Companies must apply for a listing on the NYSE, and in addition to qualifying under NYSE standards, a company must register the securities under the Securities Exchange Act 1934 before they can be admitted to dealings on the exchange.

Although it is possible for a non-US company's shares to be traded on the NYSE, many such companies prefer to create American Depository Receipts (ADRs). The advantages of ADRs are that:

- the company does not have to issue a separate class of dollar-denominated shares, but

- US investors invest in ADRs in dollars.

The company places a quantity of its equity shares with a bank, and ADRs are issued against these shares. For example, a UK company might place 10 million shares of £1 in safekeeping, and a quantity of dollar-denominated ADRs will be issued against these shares. The UK company will pay dividends in sterling, but the sterling dividends will be converted and paid to ADR holders in dollars. The US depository bank, without charge to ADR holders, provides services such as dividend payments, transfer of ownership, and distribution of the company's financial statements.

If a company chooses to list ADRs on the NYSE, they must be sponsored by an NYSE member firm. ADRs also can be listed on other US exchanges, such as Nasdaq.

Nasdaq
Nasdaq was an over-the-counter securities system introduced in the US in 1971, and called the National Association of Securities Dealers Automated Quotation. It has since changed its name to the Nasdaq Stock Market.

Nasdaq is the second-largest stock market in the US. It does not have an identifiable location. Rather, it consists of a large inter-connected computer system, with participants operating from terminals and telephones in their own offices around the world.

Although it originated in the US, and most shares traded on the market are US company shares, Nasdaq is aiming to become a global stock market.

The top Nasdaq companies are listed on the Nasdaq National Market, for which there are higher listing standards, and which offers real-time trade reporting to participants. Since 1992, shares in these companies have been traded during the early morning hours in the US when the London markets are open.

A feature of Nasdaq is that it provides for secondary market trading in shares in two ways, through market makers who maintain continuous two-way prices in the stocks in which they deal, and through Electronic Communications Networks or ECNs.

Tokyo Stock Exchange

The Tokyo Stock Exchange trades a variety of securities, including shares, corporate bonds and government bonds (JGBs).

Shares are traded on a board lot system. A board lot is a unit pack of shares, and the size of a board lot varies according to the price of a share. Trading is by means of an electronic order-driven system, the Computer-assisted Order Routing and Execution System (CORES).

The settlement of JGB transactions is in real time. Real-time gross settlement involves transactions being settled as they take place. Buyers do not get a few days' credit, as with the settlement of securities transactions in most stock markets around the world.

Although the Tokyo market remains very large, it has been affected by the collapse of Japanese share prices and the current struggling state of the Japanese economy.

Hong Kong Stock Exchange

The Hong Kong Stock Exchange is another major stock exchange in Asia, trading shares, bonds and a variety of other financial securities. Like Tokyo, trading in Hong Kong is on a board lot system, and there is an order-driven trading system, the Automatic Order Matching and Execution System (AMS). Orders are entered into the system either through terminals in the trading hall of the exchange, or from off-floor terminals in the offices of exchange participants.

Exchange trades are settled under the Continuous Net Settlement System (CNS), whereby the Hong Kong Clearing House becomes the counterparty to every buy and sell transaction on the exchange. The exchange therefore guarantees performance of every transaction to the buyer and the seller.

Settlement of transactions is the responsibility of CCASS clearing services that provide a book-entry system of electronic records of share ownership. Because of the central counterparty system used by the exchange, CCASS is able to offer a netting system of settlements to exchange participants.

London Stock Exchange

The London Stock Market provides a secondary market for trading in UK government securities (gilts) as well as a market for company shares, some warrants and corporate bonds. The exchange operates two markets, a main market for fully listed companies and a second tier market for small companies, called the Alternative Investment Market or AIM.

A number of foreign company shares are listed on the London Exchange whose historic pre-eminence as the leading stock market in Europe has been challenged by the Deutsche Börse in Frankfurt and Euronext.

Frankfurt Stock Exchange

Frankfurt is the largest of the German stock exchanges within the Deutsche Börse. Shares in the largest companies are listed in the first segment of companies, the Amtlicher Handel. There is also a second and a third segment of shares. After the main segment the most significant part of the German stock market is the Neuer Markt, a stock market for new, high-growth companies.

Trading on the exchange is now largely by electronic trading system (Xetra). There are Designated Sponsors who undertake to facilitate electronic trading by quoting bid and ask prices in shares for which they have been designated as sponsors.

Settlement of transactions is through the Clearstream clearing and settlement system.

International Capital Markets

The international capital markets serve the same purpose as the domestic markets, to bring together investors with organizations wishing to raise funds. A global offering is an international issue of shares or bonds, via a lead management bank, to investors in several different financial centers around the world.

International capital markets developed, like the eurocurrency markets for bank deposits, from the existence of offshore funds in major traded currencies, and the willingness of investors to put this money into equities or bonds.

Offshore funds are funds held in a currency outside the currency's country of origin. If they are held in a bank account, they are referred to as eurocurrency deposits. The prefix euro gained acceptance because offshore funds were at one time predominantly dollars held on deposit with banks in Europe. These were called eurodollars to distinguish them from domestic dollars held on deposit with banks in the US.

- Eurobonds is a term that was given to long-term debt securities issued and traded on the international markets. The creation of the euro currency has meant that the term is no longer widely used because of the potential for confusion between eurobonds meaning international bonds and euro bonds, meaning bonds denominated in euros.
- Commercial paper is a short-term debt instrument, but CP programs can be established for a number of years, with successive issues (and repayments) of CP within that period. For example, a company might arrange a $20 million CP program, under which it can issue short-dated CP up to a total value of $20 million at any time. If the full $20 million is needed for several years, the company would issue CP at the start of the program with a maturity of one year for example. On maturity, the issue would be rolled over for a further year, by redeeming the maturing first issue with the proceeds of another CP issue. Issues can be rolled over in this way for the

full term of the program if required. Eurocommercial paper (ECP) is CP issued and traded on the international markets, as distinct from the domestic US market.

● Euroequities are ordinary shares issued in several international centers with an international secondary market.

International Bonds

International bonds are bonds that, when issued, are sold and traded in more than one country. The bonds are sold by an international syndicate of banks, rather than through the issue mechanisms of domestic stock exchanges. Bonds may be denominated in any freely traded currency, but the major currencies of denomination are dollars and euros.

International bond issues may be categorized according to the currency of denomination. For example, a number of bond issues are denominated in sterling, and a small number of banks specialize in these issues. Consequently you may come across the term sterling bond markets, although they are really a part of the overall international bond markets.

International bonds are long-term loans raised by international companies or other institutions in several countries at the same time. The term of a bond issue typically is five to ten years. There are also a few undated or perpetual bonds.

Most international bonds are issued in bearer form that can be attractive to investors wishing to retain anonymity. Bearer securities are also administratively easier to sell in a secondary market than registered securities.

The Eurobond market began in the 1960s, in the days of fixed exchange rates, the Bretton Woods system when the dollar was on the gold standard. In 1963, the US government introduced an Interest Equalization Tax that was a surtax on bonds issued by foreign issuers in the US domestic bond market. The recognition that offshore dollars (eurodollars) could be obtained easily outside the US without paying this tax led to the first eurobond issue (the $15 million Autostrade issue, to finance building of the Italian roadway system). Other issues followed.

In 1968, faced with the high costs of the Vietnam war and a balance-of-trade deficit, the US government decided to reduce the flow of dollars out of the country by liberalizing the overseas borrowing rules for US companies. It became easier and cheaper for US companies to borrow abroad to finance overseas investments, and as a consequence, large US companies started to issue eurobonds in a big way.

Primary issues of international bonds in Europe are regulated by an organization of market intermediaries, the International Primary Market Association (IPMA) that issues guidelines that members are expected to follow. For example IPMA has developed standard documentation and procedures for market issues. The secondary market in international securities is also self-regulated, with regulations, an electronic system for trade matching and reporting (Trax) and an electronic system (Coredeal) being provided by the International Securities Market Association (ISMA).

An international syndicate handles a eurobond issue. Bonds are issued on behalf of government agencies, financial institutions, multinational companies and large corporations. Issues normally are placed, i.e. the lead manager arranging the issue will find banks and other financial institutions that will underwrite and/or sell the issue.

Example
A large UK-registered multinational company might make a dollar bond issue in the European and US markets that could be listed on the London Stock Exchange and the New York Stock Exchange. The issue in Europe would be placed by a lead bank, assisted by a syndicate of other selling banks, with a number of European and other institutional investors. Thereafter the bonds would be bought and sold internationally in the secondary markets of different countries, with the lead bank and possibly other banks acting as a market maker quoting prices, or as a broker-dealer.

The London Stock Exchange and the Luxembourg exchange are the principal centers for listing European international bond issues, but this does not put a geographical limitation on where the bonds can be traded. London-listed bonds, for example, can be traded throughout Europe.

Eurocommercial paper (ECP)

The Eurocommercial paper market, after growing rapidly in the 1980s, was hit severely by the withdrawal of several major intermediaries between 1987 and 1992. Currently, they are not widely used to raise new capital, although they could return to favor at some time in the future.

Euroequity

An international equity issue (or euroequity issue) is an issue of new equity shares that are placed with investors by lead managers in several different European and other countries. An international issue can occur at the same time as an issue on the domestic stock market.

Euroequities should be fungible with similar shares issued by the company in its domestic stock market. A security is fungible if it can take the place of or be replaced by another. Shares in ABCD Corporation, for example, that are traded in London should be fungible with shares traded in Frankfurt for example. However, the purpose of an international equity market is to create demand for the shares in several countries. Issuers and their lead managers therefore try to ensure that shares are sold to long-term investors, and do not flow back to investors in the issuer's own country in secondary-market trading after the issue has taken place, that is, in the after market.

Market Prices and Yields

It is important to have a basic understanding of market prices for securities. Prices help to determine the size of the return or yield to investors. Market prices and yields for existing issues in the secondary market also affect the price at which new securities can be issued. The purpose of this chapter is first to consider how prices are determined, and subsequently what causes them to move up or down.

Market Makers and Bid-Offer Spreads

A market maker is a dealer who, in a quote-driven trading system, will continually quote two-way prices for an issue of securities, a bid price and an offer or ask price, and who is willing to deal at those prices. The bid price is the price at which the market maker will buy the security, and the offer price is the market maker's selling price. The difference or spread between the two prices if market prices remain static, represents the market maker's profit. The financial press reports the mid-market price of a security, the average of the bid and offer prices.

Market making is an intermediary function, the matching of buyers and sellers of a security. In a liquid market, however, the market maker will not seek an exact match of sellers with buyers, but will hold a quantity of the security on its own account. The quantity that it holds will increase when there are more sellers than buyers of the security, and will fall when buyers exceed sellers. The market maker's holding can be regulated by changing the bid and offer prices, to attract more buyers or sellers or, on occasion, to deter sellers.

Example

Alpha Securities is a market maker in the shares of a company, Omega. Alpha currently holds 40,000 Omega shares on its own account, and is quoting prices of 325-335¢ per share. A customer has telephoned and arranged to sell 50,000 Omega shares to Alpha.

Analysis

Alpha will buy the 50,000 shares at the quoted price of 325. Its own holding of Omega shares therefore will increase to 90,000, and it probably will wish to sell some of these quickly.

If Alpha cannot find a willing buyer at 335, it might reduce its prices. Suppose that Alpha reduces its prices for Omega shares to 320-330 per share, and is able to sell 50,000 shares to another customer at 330.

As a result of these transactions, Alpha will make a profit of $2,500, 5¢ per share (330 - 325) on buying and reselling the 50,000 Omega shares.

When a security is traded in large amounts and the market for the security is liquid, a market maker can quote prices on a narrow spread. Higher bid prices and lower offer prices favor the market maker's clients, and should help to encourage liquidity in the market.

Example

Beta Securities makes a market in the shares of two companies, Sierra and Tango. The market for shares in Sierra is very liquid and Beta is quoting prices of 550-552¢. The market for shares in Tango is not liquid, and Beta quotes prices of 400-425¢.

On a single day when these quoted prices are not altered, Beta turns over (buys and sells) two million Sierra shares and 10,000 Tango shares.

Analysis

Beta's trading profits are as follows:

| Sierra shares | (2 million x 2¢ per share) | $40,000 |
| Tango shares | (10,000 x 25¢ per share) | $ 2,500 |

Although the spread on Sierra's prices is much lower, it is much more profitable to trade in Sierra shares because of the larger volume of transactions. At the same time, investors who sell and buy Sierra shares through Beta can benefit from the narrow spread on the quoted prices.

Prices in an Order-Driven System

In an order-driven system there are no market makers. Instead, some intermediaries undertake to maintain a liquid market in the securities by dealing on its own account in the shares whenever necessary. This means that if orders are input to the system for which an automatic match cannot be found, the dealer-broker might decide to transact the order with the other party on its own account. In deciding which orders to transact, the broker-dealer will seek to push prices up or down, according to the strength of supply or demand for the shares.

Influences on Price

Prices quoted by intermediaries fluctuate according to supply and demand in the market, i.e. according to the prices at which holders of the security are willing to sell and would-be investors are willing to buy. An investor can improve the return by purchasing at the right time when prices are lower, and by selling when prices have reached a temporary peak. Investment advisers and analysts can give recommendations on when is a good time to buy or sell.

Although market prices fluctuate continually, there are various factors that create an underlying volume of supply and demand, and determine what buyers will pay or what sellers will accept for securities. The key factors are:

- expected return from the security
- expected return from similar securities in the market

- perceived risk, and
- liquidity.

Expected Returns

The expected return, in money terms, varies according to the type of security. For bonds, the return consists of regular interest payments and the payment of the principal at maturity. For equity shares, return takes the form of dividends and the eventual selling price, should the shareholder eventually decide to sell. When a shareholder sells shares, however, the buyer is purchasing a future stream of dividends, and the selling price will reflect what the buyer is willing to pay for this expectation of future dividends. The return from convertible loan stock is interest until the loan stock is converted into shares, and dividends thereafter.

Ignoring risk and liquidity as factors that help to determine price, investors will pay more for bigger financial returns, i.e. for more interest or dividends. For example, investors will pay more for bonds with a coupon rate of 7% than for bonds with a 4% coupon because the return is higher.

Perceived Risk

Relatively few investments are risk-free. Issuers of debt securities could default on interest payments or the payment of the debt principal at maturity. Expected dividends on shares could be lower than anticipated, for example, because of a drop in the company's trading profits and a consequent decision by its board of directors to cut the dividend. When investors expect dividends to grow, there is a risk of disappointment that the actual growth rate will be less than anticipated.

The size of return required by investors will vary according to the perceived risk. A lower yield will be obtained, for example, for a risk-free investment, such as US Treasury bonds, than for the unsecured bond of a company. Yields on corporate bonds usually will be less than returns on equity shares, allowing for anticipated dividend growth and share price increases, because equity is a riskier investment. Interest is paid before dividends, and dividends, in the long term at least, depend on the company's profitability that is difficult to predict with confidence.

Foreign investors are less likely to invest in securities denominated in a currency that is perceived as weak and likely to depreciate in value. One of the reasons why a stable exchange rate is desirable is because it reduces currency risk for foreign investors, and encourages more widespread investment.

Liquidity
Investors normally will pay more for a liquid stock than for illiquid securities, because of the greater flexibility of being able to sell all or part of an investment without difficulty and at any time.

In some capital markets, liquidity varies over time. An organization wishing to raise new capital will prefer to issue securities in a market it believes to be liquid, where it can obtain a better issue price, than in an illiquid one.

Small company shares might be traded in the stock market on a matched bargain basis, so that an intermediary will agree to trade only in those shares for which a buyer can be found shares. The market for such shares is thin and illiquid. Consequently prices will be lower, to give investors a higher return.

Bond Prices

The market price of bonds and other debt securities is determined by the future income stream from the securities and the interest rate or yield that investors require. For example, if a company issues ten-year sterling bonds, redeemable at par value, with a coupon rate of 8% per annum and interest payable every six months, the issue price of the bonds (per £100 nominal value) will be at the market's valuation of an income stream of £4 every six months for ten years plus £100 at the end of ten years.

The price will give the investor a gross redemption yield on the bonds. If, for example, investors require a redemption yield of 6.5% per annum, the market price of the bonds would be the value of the future stream of interest payments and principal repayment over the ten years, discounted at a rate of 6.5% per annum.

Although discounting arithmetic is beyond the scope of this book, a pricing example is provided to illustrate how it works.

Example

Gamma, a large company, is planning the issue of five-year dollar-denominated notes. These will pay a coupon rate of 7%, and interest will be paid annually. The notes will be redeemed at par after five years.

Gamma's management believes that investors will buy the notes at a price that gives them a gross redemption yield of 6.5% per annum.

Analysis

To give investors a yield of 6.5%, the issue price for each $100 of the notes must be equal to the discounted value of $7 interest per annum for five years and $100 after five years. The discount rate is the required investment yield of 6.5% or 0.065.

Year	Item	Amount per $100 bond $	Discount rate at 6.5%	Present value $
1	Interest	7	$\dfrac{1}{(1.065)^1}$	6.57
2	Interest	7	$\dfrac{1}{(1.065)^2}$	6.17
3	Interest	7	$\dfrac{1}{(1.065)^3}$	5.79
4	Interest	7	$\dfrac{1}{(1.065)^4}$	5.44
5	Interest	7	$\dfrac{1}{(1.065)^5}$	5.11
5	Principal	100	$\dfrac{1}{(1.065)^1}$	72.99
Total value				102.07

75

An issue of the 7% bonds at a price of 102.07 would give investors a redemption yield of 6.5% on the bonds.

Yield on Bonds

The gross redemption yield from a bond is the return, expressed as a rate of interest, that will be obtained on the bond over its term to maturity, at its current market value.

Example

A ten-year government bond is issued at a price of 98.20, that is $98.20 per $100 nominal value of bonds. Interest of 7% is paid annually and the bond is redeemable at par after ten years.

Analysis

The redemption yield on the bond is the overall rate of interest that an investor in $100 of bonds will receive for the purchase cost of $98.20 and before tax on his/her income, from interest payments of $7 per annum for ten years and a payment of principal of $100 on redemption at the end of ten years.

Investment cost now	98.20
Years 1-7 Interest	7.00 per annum
Year 7 Redemption value	100.00

The yield, that can be calculated using discount arithmetic or a suitable calculator, is about 7.25%.

Estimating a Fixed-Rate Bond Yield

A *rough estimate* of the yield on bonds, particularly bonds with a long-time to redemption, for example 10 years or more, can be made by ignoring the redemption value. The formula for this estimate is:

$$\text{Yield} = \frac{\text{Annual Interest}}{\text{Market Price}} \times 100\%$$

Example

The interest rate on a bond with 15 years to redemption is 6%. The market price of the bond is 101.50.

Analysis

The redemption yield on the bond is *approximately*:

$$\frac{6}{101.50} \times 100\% = 5.9\%$$

Using the same simplified formula, a suitable market price for a long-term bond can be estimated from the annual interest payment and the required interest yield.

$$\text{Market Price} = \frac{\text{Annual Interest (Coupon rate)}}{\text{Required Yield (\%)}} \times 100$$

Example

A government is planning the issue of 20-year bonds bearing a coupon rate of 5.5% per annum. The yield that investors currently require is about 6%.

Analysis

The approximate issue price to give investors a 6% yield is

$$\frac{5.50}{6.00} \times 100\% = 91.67$$

Movements in Interest Rates (Yields) and Changes in Bond Prices

When interest rates in the capital markets go up or down, the market value of fixed-rate bonds already in issue also will change. This is because the bonds, having been issued at a fixed rate, will continue to pay the same fixed amount of interest, but the return required by investors has changed. Suppose, for example, that an investor holds $100 of 20-year bonds paying interest of 6% per annum. The current market yield on bonds is also 6%, and the bonds therefore have a market value of $100 (par).

If interest rates now go down to 5%, the investor will still receive interest of $10 per annum on the bonds. However at the new market interest rate (investment yield) of 5%, bonds with a market value of $100 will be expected to yield annual interest of only $5. Bonds paying

$6 therefore must now be worth more than $100, and the bond price will go up. The new price can be roughly estimated from the formula:

$$\text{Market Value} = \frac{\text{Interest per annum on bonds}}{\text{Market Rate of Interest}}$$

In the example above, the new market price of the bonds when bond yields change from 6% (0.06) to 5% (0.05) will be *approximately*:

$$\frac{\$6}{0.05} = 120.00$$

While the formula gives only an approximation of the market price, it does illustrates the key principle that when market interest rates go down, prices of existing bonds go up. Conversely, when interest rates go up, bond prices fall.

Interest Rate Changes and Bond Prices

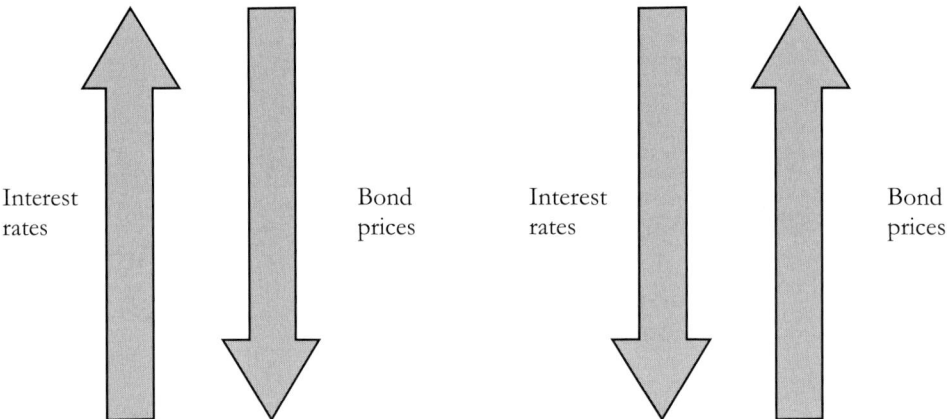

Interest rates   Bond prices   Interest rates   Bond prices

Variable-Rate Bonds (Floating-Rate Notes)
The market price of variable-rate bonds normally should remain close to par, because the interest paid to investors will rise or fall in step with movements in market rates of interest. However, if there is a change in the perceived risk to investors, and investors therefore require a higher or lower yield to compensate them for the risk, the market price will change.

Example

Victor, a large international company, has issued floating-rate notes that pay interest at 50 basis points (0.50%) above six-month LIBOR. The notes, that were issued at par, have a remaining maturity of nearly ten years. Their current market value is par.

Victor's profitability unexpectedly declines, and investors reassess the company's credit standing. In view of the higher risk from investing in Victor's debt capital, investors would wish to receive a margin of 100 basis points over LIBOR. Six-month LIBOR currently is 4.5% per annum.

Analysis

The notes are paying 0.5% over LIBOR (5.0% currently) but investors require 1% over LIBOR (5.5% currently). The market price of the notes will fall, possibly from a par value of 100 to about:

$$\frac{5.0}{5.50} \times 100 = 90.91$$

Pricing a Bond Issue

At the time of a new issue of bonds, it is important to select the issue price and coupon rate of interest. If the bonds are to be issued at par, the coupon rate should reflect the interest yield that investors will expect to receive. Bonds need not be issued at par, however, but the coupon rate of interest must still be sufficient to attract investors to buy the bonds at the issue price.

- If the coupon interest rate is generous in relation to the issue price, investors will be keen to buy at that price. After the issue, the price of the bonds will rise in the secondary market.
- If the coupon rate is too low, or the issue price is too high, investors will be reluctant to buy at that price and the issue will be under-subscribed. In the subsequent secondary market, the

bond price will fall below the issue price.

Example

An investment bank lead-manages a £250-million international bond issue for a UK telecommunications group. The ten-year bonds pay a coupon rate of 4.75%, and are priced aggressively at 99.60. At this price, the bonds offered a yield of 40 basis points (0.40%), higher than the yield on comparable UK government bonds.

The pricing is critical to the success of the issue. Banks in the underwriting syndicate for the issue might be concerned about a lack of investor interest at this price, and as underwriters, fear being required to buy up a large quantity of unsold bonds. If the yield had been made a little higher to attract buyers, possibly 43-45 basis points above UK government bond yields, the bonds might have succeeded in attracting investors.

If, in the event, there is some difficulty in selling the bonds at the issue price, a quantity of bonds probably will be taken up by the underwriters, and the market price of the bonds will fall below the issue price.

Share Prices

There are differing views about how shares are valued by the market. One view is that share prices have an intrinsic or fundamental value, and that shares can be valued on fundamentals by discounting a stream of expected future dividend payments at the rate of return required by shareholders.

It is useful to be aware of two formulae for pricing shares on fundamentals. Both formulae use simplifying assumptions about dividends, but are nevertheless useful for reference when assessing share values.

Formula 1

If a company is expected to pay the same amount of dividend per share

every year into the foreseeable future, with no dividend growth, the
formula for valuing the share on fundamentals is:

$$P = \frac{d}{r}$$

where P is the share price

d is the annual dividend (in pence)

r is the shareholders' required rate of return, expressed as a
proportion, e.g. 10% = 0.10, 8% = 0.08, etc.

Formula 2

If the company is expected to achieve dividend growth at a constant
annual rate of growth over the years, the formula for the fundamental
value of the share will be

$$P = \frac{d(1+g)}{(r-g)}$$

where P is the share price

d is the most recent annual dividend, in cents

r is the shareholders' required rate of return

g is the expected annual growth in dividends, expressed as a
proportion, e.g. 2% = 0.02

d (1 + g) is therefore next year's expected dividend.

Example

Indigo is a company whose shares have a liquid market. The most recent
annual dividend, interim and final, was 15 cents per share. Shareholders
in Indigo expect an annual return of 9%.

Analysis

If Indigo is expected to maintain its dividend unchanged at 10 cents, the
share price, based on fundamentals, should be:

$$P = \frac{15 \text{ cents}}{0.09} = 166.7 \text{ cents}$$

If, however, Indigo is expected to achieve an annual growth rate in dividends of five per cent, the dividend next year will be 15.75 cents (15 x 1.05). The share price, based on fundamentals, would be:

$$P = \frac{15.75 \text{ cents}}{(0.09 - 0.05)} = 393.75 \text{ cents}$$

Validity of the Fundamental Theory of Share Values
If the theory is correct, that shares have a fundamental value based on market expectations of future dividends, the price of any share should be predictable provided that:

- all investors have the same information about a company's expected future profits and dividends
- they share the same expectations, and
- the return required by shareholders is known.

So is the theory correct? Are share prices predictable?

In concept the theory could seem valid. A share's price should reflect a current valuation of an expected future income stream from dividends because the value of any investment must be related to the return that investors expect to get from it. In reality, however, the prices of widely traded shares fluctuate continually.

The validity of the theory was challenged by the sharp fall in share prices, particularly on Wall Street, in the crash of October 1987. There was a sudden and very sharp fall in share prices on all the stock exchanges of the world, on average by 20% to 40%, but some share prices fell by 50% or more. The crash could not be explained by fundamental analysis because there was no obvious change in expectations about company profits and dividends.

Random Walk Theory of Share Values
A refinement of the fundamental theory of share values is that although share prices have an intrinsic or fundamental value, this value will alter as new information becomes available to the market. The behavior of investors in response to new information as it arrives is such that the

actual share price will fluctuate from day to day around the intrinsic value, but in a random manner that cannot be predicted until it has happened.

Prices continually move in response to new information coming to the market, it is argued, because the market is efficient and new information is disseminated quickly. An efficient market is one in which investors are able to price shares fairly and alter prices in immediate response to new information as it is obtained. The market prices of all the securities traded on an efficient market will reflect all available information. The efficiency of a stock market depends on the widespread availability of information about companies, their shares and market conditions. This information is what market makers and other financial institutions provide for their clients and for the general investing public. The random walk theory therefore can be used to argue that fundamental analysis of share prices is valid in an efficient market, although share price movements will be continual and unpredictable.

The Practical Value of the Fundamental Share Price Theory
Although the fundamental theory of share values might seem valid, and price fluctuations can be explained by shareholder responses to new information in an efficient stock market, the theory has little practical value as a predictor of future price movements. Analyzing fundamentals can help an analyst to judge whether a share's current price is too high or too low, but it cannot predict which direction the price will move next.

Investors and investment analysts want to be able to predict future price movements, particularly changing trends when prices will start to rise or fall, and fundamental analysis is inadequate for such predictions. Some analysts, known as chartists, attempt to predict price movements by technical analysis.

Charting (Technical Analysis)

Chartists or technical analysts predict share price movements by assuming that past price patterns will be repeated. There is no real theoretical justification for this approach, but it can at times be spectacularly successful. Studies have suggested that the degree of success by chartists is greater than could be expected merely from luck or chance.

Chartists do not attempt to predict every price change. Primarily they are interested in trend reversals, for example when the price of a share has been rising for several months but should soon start to fall. There are several features of charts that are considered important. These include:

- trend lines
- resistance levels
- double tops and double bottoms
- head and shoulders patterns.

Resistance Level

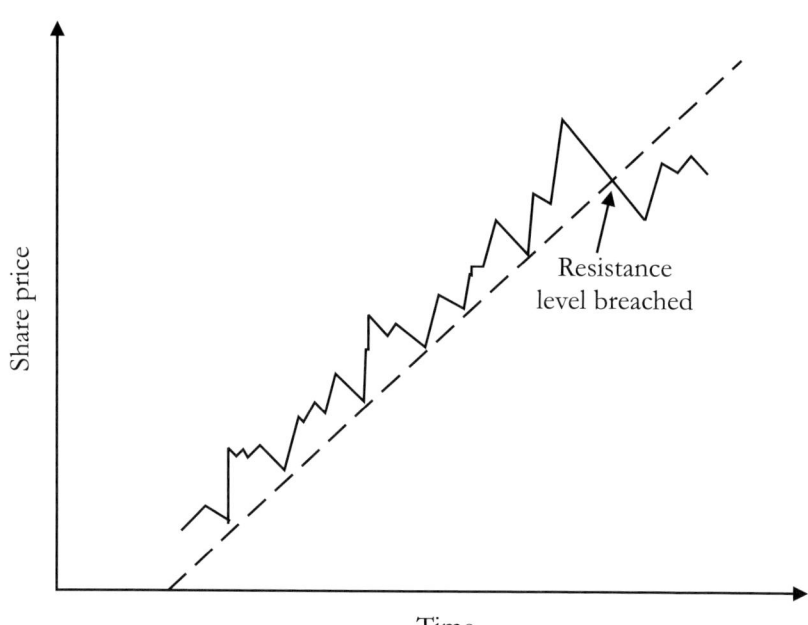

In the diagram on page 84, the share price is on a rising trend. A *resistance level* is a level above which or below which the price does not appear to go. In the diagram, the dotted line represents a lower resistance level on a rising trend. Many of the price troughs lie on this line, but when the resistance level is reached, the price rises again. Eventually, however, the resistance level is breached. To a chartist this breach would be a good indication that the trend has now been reversed, that the upward movement in prices has ended and a decline in the price should now be expected.

A *double top* is a maximum price resistance level that is reached twice before the share price starts on a downward trend. Suppose that the price of a share rises steadily for some time then fell temporarily as some investors sold to realize profits, and subsequently rose to its maximum level for a second time before starting to fall again.

This is a double top price pattern. The chartist would predict that the price trend has reversed, and a fall in the price, perhaps as steep as the earlier price, should be expected. A typical double top is shown in the diagram below.

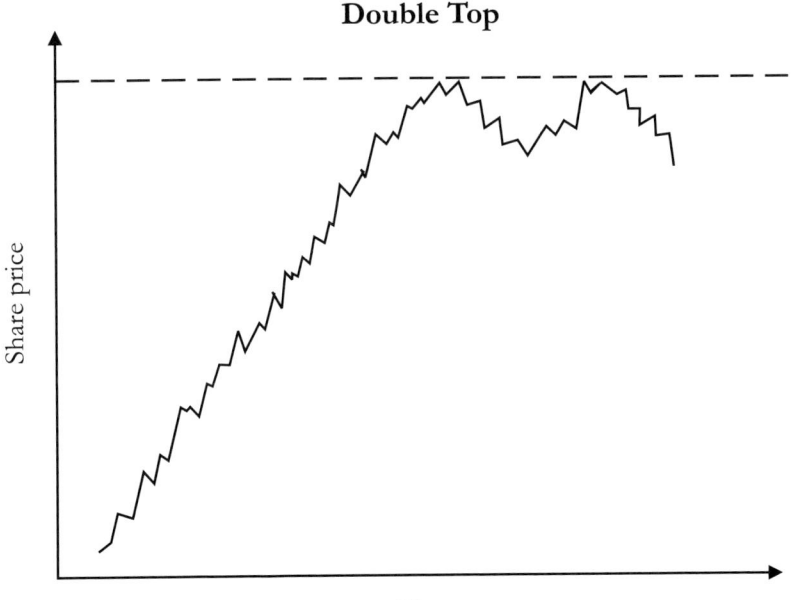

Double Top

Another indication of a price trend reversal is the *head and shoulders pattern*. This is illustrated in the diagram below. Its name should be apparent from the shape of the graph.

Head and Shoulders

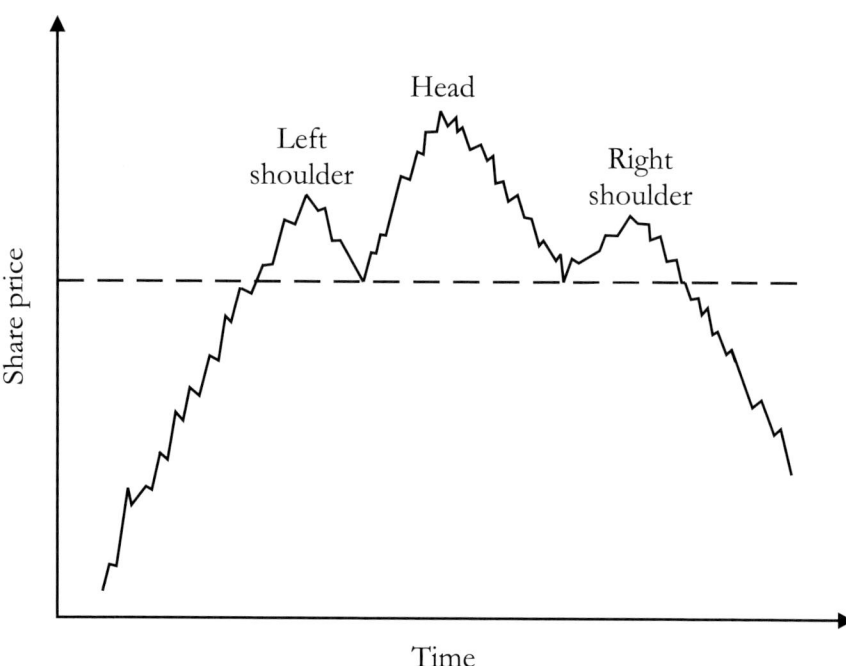

In the graph, the price has risen for some time before, at the left shoulder, profit-taking caused the price to drop. The price has then risen steeply again to a peak level, the head, before more profit-taking causes the price to drop to more or less the same level as before the most recent rise. A neck line can be drawn between these two similar price levels. The price then rises again but the gains are not as great as at the head. When it reaches the right shoulder, the price falls once more towards the neck. This will suggest to the chartist that the upward trend is over and that a sharp price fall could be imminent. The breach of the neckline is an indication to sell the shares.

An inverse head and shoulders can be interpreted in a similar manner.

Moving averages can help the chartist to examine overall trends. For example, a chartist could calculate and plot moving averages of share prices for 20 days, 60 days and 240 days. The 20-day figures will give a reasonable representation of the actual movement in share prices after eliminating day-to-day fluctuations. The other two moving averages can give a good idea of longer-term trends.

Example
It is interesting to look at the share price index for the London stock market, the FT- UK Actuaries All-Share Index leading up to the stock market crash in October 1987. Fundamental analysis of share prices could have indicated that the general level of prices was too high, but could not have predicted the sudden crash. A study of a chart, however, could have given some warning of a steep price fall.

FT UK Actuaries All-Share Index

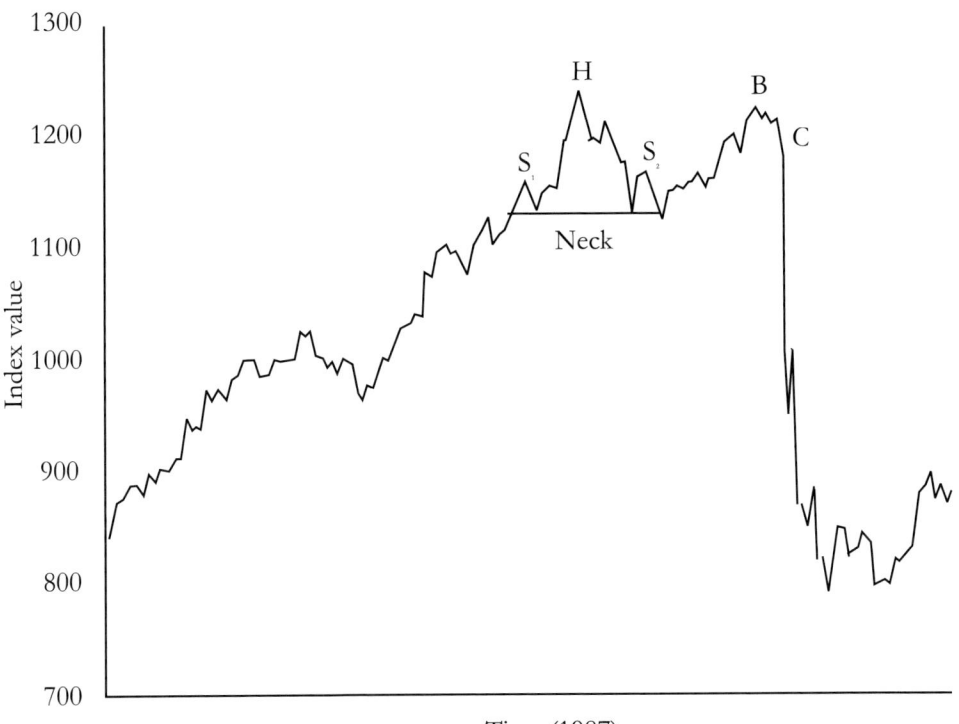

Around the peak in the index level at 1239, on July 16 1987, a head-and-shoulders pattern is discernible, marked on the chart with a neckline.

For a head-and-shoulders pattern to be fully formed, however, the requirement is that after the basic pattern of shoulder-head-shoulder has been formed, the price should be at least 3% below the neckline for one day, or at least 1% below the neckline for two days. In August 1987, this did not quite happen, and the price index rose again, to 1222 on October 5. After October 5, it began a slow decline, and an alternative pattern, the double top, with peaks at 1239 on July 16 and 1222 on October 5, becomes visible. The sharp drop in the index, to below 800, began on Black Monday, October 19.

A chartist approach can be particularly effective for individual blue chip stocks, i.e. shares in companies with a low risk of deterioration in earnings. These can produce a repetition of identifiable pricing patterns and investors can buy at the bottom and sell at the top of pricing ranges.

Prices for Small Companies' Shares

The market for shares in many small companies can be relatively inactive. Trades could be occasional, but when they do occur also could be quite large. An investment risk with such shares is that a single transaction could move the market price substantially. For example, if a shareholder wishes to sell a large block of shares, there might not be a willing buyer except at a price well below the currently quoted market price.

The main market maker or broker dealer for shares in a small company could try to limit this risk by cultivating a group of institutional investors who would be willing, given assurances about the long-term growth and dividend prospects, to:

- buy blocks of shares that the market maker wishes to sell, and
- sell blocks of shares when the market maker needs some for a new buyer.

This arrangement can help to stabilize the share price and prevent the volatility that would otherwise unsettle and deter investors.

Entitlement to Dividends and Interest

It is useful to be aware of the rules applying to the entitlement to dividends and interest when securities are traded on a secondary market. When a buyer acquires securities in a secondary-market transaction, it is important to establish clearly whether the next payment of dividends or interest should be made to the buyer, or whether the seller should receive this payment. In other words, has the sale price included the right to receive the next dividend/interest payment or not?

The problem is particular to *registered securities*. The dividend or interest for bearer securities is payable to the holder of the interest or dividend coupon, or whoever is the recorded owner of the securities in the book entry system.

Cum Dividend and Ex Dividend
Shares might be traded between the time a company announces a dividend and the time the dividend is paid. When a buyer acquires the right to receive the dividend, the shares are bought *cum div*. When the seller retains the right to receive the next dividend, the shares are sold *ex div*.

There are stock exchange rules to establish whether the entitlement to the dividend, when it is eventually paid, belongs to the seller of the shares, i.e. the former owner, or the buyer, the current owner.

Rules vary from one stock exchange to another. In the UK, for example, the London Stock Exchange specifies the dates on which shares switch from being traded *cum div* to *ex div*.

On the *ex div* date, a share price is adjusted downwards by the amount of dividend payable because buyers are no longer acquiring the dividend rights.

Example

A UK company with shares listed on the London Stock Exchange announced a final dividend of 10p per share on December 15, payable on April 15. On January 3, the last day of trading *cum rights*, the mid-market share price was 205p.

On January 4, the first day of trading ex rights, the stock exchange would adjust its official opening price of the shares from 205p to 195p, to allow for the dividend of 10p that will no longer belong to a buyer of the shares. If the share price remains at 205p during the day, the financial press would report an increase of 10p in the share price on the day. Sellers still would be getting the same price as on the day before, but unlike sellers on January 3, would now be entitled to receive the 10p dividend in April.

Accrued Interest, Cum Int and Ex Int

Bonds differ from equity shares because the amount and dates of future interest payments should always be known. For example, 6% bonds might pay a coupon rate of 3% every six months, and the interest payment dates would be on specific dates each year. In contrast, the amount of the next equity dividend is unknown until the company makes a dividend announcement.

When bonds are traded, they are sold either:

- cum interest, with the buyer obtaining the right to receive the next six-monthly interest payment up to a certain threshold date, or
- ex interest, with the seller retaining the right to receive this interest after this date.

Bonds may be sold ex interest in the period just before an interest payment date. The rules of the stock market will determine whether bonds will be sold cum or ex interest.

Interest builds up or accrues over time, between payment dates. For example, suppose that interest on 8% Treasury Stock is paid six monthly, on April 30 and October 31 each year. In the period between May 1 and October 31, every £100 of stock will be earning interest at 8% per annum. By October 31, interest (for six months) of £4 will have accrued and will be paid.

If stock is traded at any time between May 1 and October 31, there will be unpaid accrued interest. If £100 of the stock is traded on July 31, for example, there will be three months' accrued interest of £2.

When government stocks are sold, the accrued interest is added to the price that the buyer pays. The traded price is a clean price, without any accrued interest, but on settlement, the buyer pays the clean price plus the accrued interest. Continuing the example of the 8% Treasury Stock, if £100 of stock is sold at 101.5 on July 31, the buyer will pay the clean price of £101.50 plus accrued interest of £2 giving a total price of £103.50.

Summary

Market prices are determined predominantly by expected returns, perceived risk and market liquidity. Continual fluctuations in price can be expected in an efficient market, reflecting altered perceptions arising from new information about individual companies and industrial sectors, prospects for the economy or political developments affecting economic or regulatory conditions.

There is a close link between movements in market prices and interest-rate changes. When interest-rates rise, the price of bonds currently in issue will fall.

Higher interest rates also will affect share prices, partly because prospects for corporate profitability will be poorer, but mainly because shareholders, like bondholders, will now expect a higher yield on their investments. When higher yields are required, prices inevitably must fall.

There is also a close link between bond prices and share prices because these market are alternative homes for investment funds. In times of high inflation shares are preferred over fixed-rate bonds because the value of interest is eroded by inflation. In times of low inflation, bonds are favored. When a recession is anticipated along with a fall in the rate of inflation, there is switching from shares to bonds. At the end of the recession, in anticipation of higher inflation, there is an opposite move from bonds into shares. Although institutional investors hold both bonds and equities they can and do radically adjust their weightings of each in their investment portfolio.

6

New Issues

The Relationship Between the Primary and Secondary Markets

A stock exchange can provide both a primary market for new issues and a secondary market for subsequent trading. In the US, to make a public issue of shares or debt capital, the issuer must be registered with the Securities and Exchange Commission (SEC). In the UK, a company issuing new shares in the primary market normally also has them admitted to trading on a stock exchange, such as the main market of the London Stock Exchange or the Alternative Investment Market, for secondary market trading. A requirement for obtaining an official listing for shares in the UK is that they should be admitted to trading on the London Stock Exchange.

In a quote-driven market, there must be market makers willing to offer continual two-way prices; otherwise the market will lack liquidity. Similarly, in an order-driven system, the market will be illiquid unless orders to buy or sell can be taken up quickly by a matching seller or buyer. Broker-dealers add liquidity to an order-driven market by dealing in shares on their own account.

It could be supposed that liquidity in the secondary markets is a problem for investors and intermediaries, but not for issuers. This, however, is not the case. Issuers must be concerned about secondary-market liquidity because without it there could be a lack of investor support for new issues in the future.

The advantage of issuing securities in the US is the liquidity of the capital market, and the large number of potential investors. This contrasts with the Japanese market and the international markets that go through cycles of liquidity and illiquidity, particularly in certain types of security such as convertible bonds, medium-term notes, commercial paper, and certain currencies including sterling.

Waiting Periods

In some markets, there are regulations about the minimum time between the issue of new securities and the first date on which they can be traded in the secondary market. This is called a waiting period.

Methods of Issuing Shares

In broad terms, there are three main ways of issuing new shares to raise capital:

- a public offering
- a placing or placement
- a rights issue.

Public Offering
A public offering is an offer to the general investing public to subscribe for a new issue of securities at a fixed offer price. The issuer usually will appoint a sponsoring securities house or investment bank to manage the issue on its behalf. A public offering by a securities house or bank on behalf of a client may be called an offer for sale.

When companies go public for the first time, a *large* issue probably will take the form of a public offering. A small issue is more likely to be a placing because the amount to be raised can be obtained more cheaply if the issuing house or other sponsoring firm approaches selected institutional investors privately.

In a public offering, the company and its advisers decide on the offer price, i.e. the price at which the shares will be offered to the public. The decision about the price will be left as late as possible. The company's investment bank or issuing house then will try to sell the shares on offer at the offer price. If the issue is underwritten, which is likely, the underwriters promise to buy any unsold shares at the offer price.

It can be difficult to decide on the price at which new shares should be offered to the general public. When share prices are buoyant, and market sentiment is optimistic, one way of trying to ensure that the issue price reflects a full value for the shares is to make an offer for sale by tender.

A minimum price for the issue is fixed and subscribers are invited to tender for shares at prices equal to or above this minimum. The shares are then allotted to subscribers at the highest price at which all will be taken up. This is known as the striking price.

Example
Alpha is a new company making its first public issue of shares. It has decided to make the issue by means of an offer for sale by tender. Its intention is to issue up to 40 million shares at a minimum price of $2.50 per share.

The following tenders have been received.

Price per share tendered $	Number of shares applied for at this price
6.00	500,000
5.50	1,000,000
5.00	3,000,000
4.50	4,500,000
4.00	11,000,000
3.50	15,000,000
3.00	25,000,000
2.50	40,000,000
	100,000,000

Analysis

Offers have been received for 100 million shares at prices ranging from $6 down to $2.50. Starting at the highest price and working down, the issuer will establish the cumulative number of shares tendered for at or above each price. This is shown in the table below.

Price per share $	Cumulative of shares applied	
6.00	500,000	
5.50	1,500,000	(500,000 + 1,000,000)
5.00	4,500,000	(1,500,000 + 3,000,000)
4.50	9,000,000	(4,500,000 + 4,500,000)
4.00	20,000,000	(9,000,000 + 11,000,000)
3.50	35,000,000	(20,000,000 + 15,000,000)
3.00	60,000,000	(35,000,000 + 25,000,000)
2.50	100,000,000	(60,000,000 + 40,000,000)

In a tender issue, if exactly 40 million shares are to be issued, the issue price in this example must be $3. This is the striking price at which the full 40 million shares can be sold. The company therefore will issue 40 million shares at $3 each, to raise $120 million ignoring issue costs.

Because 40 million shares are to be allotted, and there were applications for 60 million shares at or above the striking rice of $3, successful applicants will be allotted two-thirds of the shares for which they applied.

Offer for Sale by Tender Compared with an Auction

In an offer for sale by tender, all the shares are allotted at the same striking price. This is different from an auction issue where all the successful applicants are allotted securities at the price they bid.

In the example above, if the company had been able to issue its shares by auction, and the same bids had been received, the allotment of securities and the capital raised, would have been:

Price per share bid $	Number of shares applied for	Capital raised $ million
6.00	500,000	3.00
5.50	1,000,000	5.50
5.00	3,000,000	15.00
4.50	4,500,000	20.25
4.00	11,000,000	44.00
3.50	15,000,000	52.50
3.00	5,000,000	15.00
		155.25

Companies are unable to raise capital by auction, but governments may issue bonds by means of auction. Even though the prices bid by applicants will not vary broadly, auctions are likely to raise more capital from an issue than if the bonds are all offered at a single fixed price. Auction issues for government bonds are a common method of issue.

Placing (Placement)
A placing or placement is the selective marketing of a new issue of securities to a group of investors, usually institutional investors, at a fixed issue price. The sponsoring issuing house has the job of trying to ensure a successful issue for the securities by advising on an issue price and stimulating the interest of institutional investors in the issue.

A private placement market is one in which securities are regularly issued and sold over the counter to a fairly small group of end-investors, that is placed privately, rather than issued by open offer to the public. After the issue, there will be a secondary market in the securities.

A potential weakness of private placement can be the absence of liquidity in the secondary market, perhaps due to regulations restricting or prohibiting a secondary market in such securities. The most liquid private placement market is in the US that is accessible to foreign companies wishing to raise capital. International bonds are issued through private selling to institutional clients, and the lead manager for the issue and possibly some other banks will undertake to maintain a secondary market in the bonds after issue.

A feature of international bond issues is that the selling banks will try to gauge the strength of interest in a forthcoming issue of securities, and will discuss the issue with various clients. The response of clients will help the company and its advisers to fix the offer price for the issue.

Placings are less expensive and, subject to local regulations and stock market rules, are used for smaller issues, for example share issues by small companies. After the issue, placed shares can be admitted to the official list of securities in one or more countries, and admitted to trading on the secondary market of a stock exchange in that country.

Rights Issue

A rights issue is an issue of equity share capital in which new shares are offered to existing shareholders in proportion to the size of their existing shareholdings. (In the UK, company law gives existing equity shareholders the right to be offered new shares that the company intends to issue to raise cash although these rights may be waived with the agreement of the shareholders.)

The pattern of a rights issue normally will be as follows:

- A company announces a rights issue to raise new capital.
- The company's market sponsor (securities house) obtains underwriters for the issue so guaranteeing the issuer the capital it is trying to raise.
- In the period between the announcement of the issue and the issue closing date of between 7 and 8 weeks, rights can be traded. Shareholders can sell their rights to subscribe to the new issue.
- When the issue takes place, investors with rights to subscribe must do so by a final date. An issue is judged a success if a large proportion of shareholders exercise their rights and buy the new shares, and if the market price after the issue remains at or above the theoretical ex-rights price.

Rights issues can succeed in their objective of raising equity capital, but can be criticized in the long term if the share price falls, creating a capital loss for subscribers to the issue.

A company will be cautious about deciding to raise new capital through a share issue, particularly when there is not much investor enthusiasm for equity. It will be difficult to find underwriters for the issue unless the issue price is at a deep discount to the current market price, and a company will be reluctant to issue shares at a low price because of the adverse effect this is likely to have on market sentiment.

Timing an Issue

Timing an issue can be critical to its success. Investor sentiment can be volatile, and there will be times when issues can be made more easily, or at a better price for the issuer than at other times. On the other hand, the market can turn against new issues temporarily. For example, if there has been a series of unsuccessful and disappointing rights issues, another company coming to the market with a rights issue could have difficulty persuading shareholders or finding new investors willing enough to buy shares.

Documentation for an Issue

Documentation for an issue must be prepared for submission to the regulatory authorities and for putting to potential investors. The documentation will include some form of prospectus giving details about the issue and the issuer. National listing regulations specify how much information is required for securities that will be listed in the country concerned. The amount of information in the documentation is generally less for private placements than for public issues.

The purpose of such documentation is to:

- establish a contractual relationship between the issuer and the investor
- set out the specific terms of the issue
- identify any previous covenants given by the issuer on existing loans that could affect an investor in the new issue.

There are also national regulations about the content of investment advertisements, such as newspaper advertisements announcing a share issue and inviting applications from investors.

Underwriting an Issue

Underwriters in the capital markets are investment institutions or securities houses that undertake to purchase a specified quantity of a new issue of securities at an agreed price in the event that no one else will. In return, they receive a commission, typically between 1% and 2% of the value of the securities they are underwriting. The size of the commission depends on the perceived risk for the underwriter.

By using an underwriter the company making the issue is sure of receiving the funds it wants to raise, net of expenses. For example, a company might plan a share issue at a price of $10 per share. The company's market sponsor for the issue will underwrite much of the issue, but also could obtain sub-underwriters who will agree to purchase a quantity of the new shares at $10 in the event that there is insufficient demand for the issue in the market.

If the issue were successful, the underwriters would not have to buy the shares, and would take their commission. If the issue were a failure, the underwriters would take up their allocation of shares at $10, and hope to sell them subsequently in the secondary market or after-market, probably at a loss.

For international bond issues, underwriting is similar, except that the underwriters buy their allocation of bonds from the lead manager for the issue, and try to resell them to end-investors. If they cannot resell them, the bonds are left in their hands, although an agreement might exist to sell them back to the lead manager at a lower price.

Underwriters remove the risk of an issue being under-subscribed, but at a cost to the issuer. It is not always necessary to have an issue underwritten, and underwriting is not compulsory.

- It should be unnecessary to underwrite a placing if purchasers for the shares are arranged at an early stage in the issue process.
- An offer for sale by tender should need underwriting only if there is a risk of under-subscription, even at the minimum price.
- In theory, a rights issue should not require underwriting because new shares are being offered to existing shareholders. However, the underwriting of rights issues is usual because existing shareholders might refuse to buy the new shares that are being offered.

As an alternative to underwriting an issue, a company could choose to issue its shares at a deep discount, i.e. at a price well below the current market price, to ensure the success of the issue. Deep discounting is not usual although there have been occasional issues of shares at a deep discount that also have been underwritten at the discounted offer price.

The Issue Price

The price at which shares are offered is critical to the success of an issue. The offer price must be advertised a short time in advance, so it is fixed without certain knowledge of the condition of the market at the time applications are invited from investors. In order to safeguard the success of an issue, share prices often are set lower than they might otherwise be.

An issuing house also could deliberately try to ensure that a share price rises to a premium above its issue price soon after trading begins. A target premium of 10% or so above the issue price is fairly typical. For example, if an issuing house thinks that a fair price for a new issue is $5, it could recommend a price of $4.50 for the issue, and hope to see a 50¢ increase in price in the after-market – the secondary market following the issue.

Companies and their market sponsors also should be keen to avoid over-pricing an issue, to prevent the issue being under-subscribed, and leaving underwriters with the unwelcome task of having to buy up the unsold shares. However, if the issue price is too low, the issue will be over-subscribed and the company would have been able to raise the required capital by issuing fewer shares.

Stabilization

Stabilization is a price-supporting process, whereby a stabilizing manager, for example a market maker, undertakes to keep the price of securities stable in the after-market following an issue to prevent sharp price fluctuations. Stabilization can be used for a new issue of shares or fixed-rate bonds. Its purpose is to effect an orderly distribution of the offering. Usually the stabilization manager will be buying the security to prevent the price falling.

An intention to provide price stabilization must be notified to the market. Potential buyers should be aware that the stabilizing manager or managers may buy or sell securities to maintain the price at a level that otherwise would not prevail. Typically a stabilizing process has no set time period and may be discontinued at any time.

Other Methods of Issuing Shares

The main methods of raising new capital from share issues, as mentioned previously, are public offerings, placings and rights issues. Shares can be issued by other methods:

- as the purchase consideration in a takeover bid
- as a scrip issue (bonus issue or capitalization issue) or scrip dividend
- on conversion of convertible stock into ordinary shares
- by means of share options
- by means of share warrants.

Of these methods, new capital, cash, is raised only with options and warrants. The other methods of issue increase the number of shares but do not raise extra cash.

Share Options

A distinction must be made between share options issued by a company and share options that are traded on a stock exchange and known as traded options. Companies can issue share options to raise capital. Traded options, on the other hand, are for investment management; they are not issued by companies and are not for raising capital.

Company share options give their holder the right to buy new shares in the company at a specified exercise price at some future date. Options can be issued to employees within an employee share-option scheme. The exercise price is commonly the market price of the shares when the options were issued, or at a discount to the market price. For example, a company whose share price is $6 might grant share options to selected employees, giving them the right after a period of three years, for example, to subscribe for a specified quantity of new shares at a price of $6.

When the exercise date is reached, or between the earliest and latest exercise dates, the employees would exercise their options if the market price of the shares is above $6. When the options are exercised, the company creates new shares and allots them to the option holders at the exercise price. If the employees do not wish to hold on to their shares, they can sell them at a profit.

Company option schemes primarily are intended to reward employees if the company is successful, i.e. if its share price rises between the issue date and the exercise date for the options, but also can be a useful source of extra funds for the company.

Share Warrants (Subscription Rights)
A warrant is a right given by a company to an investor, allowing him/her to buy new shares at a future date at a fixed, pre-determined price that is called the exercise price.

Warrants usually are issued as part of a package with unsecured loan stock: an investor who buys stock also will acquire a certain number of warrants. The purpose of warrants is to make the loan stock more attractive. If the warrants are exercised, the company will issue new shares at the exercise price, and raise new capital.

Once issued, warrants are detachable from the stock and can be sold and bought separately in a secondary market before or during the exercise period. This is the period during which the right to use the warrants to subscribe for shares is allowed. The market value of warrants will depend on expectations of actual share prices in the future.

When the date for exercising the warrant is reached, the value of the warrant will be the difference between the current share price and the warrant's exercise price if one warrant entitles its holder to subscribe for one share. If the exercise price exceeds the current share price, the warrant will have no value and will not be exercised.

In secondary market trading before the exercise period, however, although the exercise price could be higher than the current share price, the warrant nevertheless could have a market value. This is because the share price is expected to rise before the exercise period is reached.

Bond Issues: International Bonds

New issues of securities in the international markets are placed by an international syndicate of banks. There is a lead manager and book runner for the issue. The lead manager puts together a syndicate of underwriters, and banks that will sell the securities to investors. The book-runner that may be the same investment bank, will co-ordinate the selling efforts.

An international bond issue is arranged as follows.

- The borrower will appoint an investment bank to lead-manage the bond issue.
- This lead-managing bank invites other banks to co-manage the issue. Each of the managing banks will expect fees, perhaps 0.5% of the total issue amount, plus expenses.
- The managing banks might try to ensure the success of the bond issue by inviting a group of banks and other financial institutions to underwrite the issue.
- Once the issue is underwritten, the managing banks will try to place the issue with a number of selling banks and other financial institutions. The selling banks usually include some of the underwriters. They receive a commission on the amount of the issue allotted to them.
- The selling banks try to place all or some of their allotment with their clients. The placing power of the selling banks is a vital factor in the successful launch of a new issue, and it is crucial that the selling banks should be able to place the bonds with willing buyers.
- To help the selling process a prospectus will be prepared for potential investors giving information about the terms and conditions of the bond, the name of the issuer and details of its business and past financial results, the purpose of the funding, and selling information.
- Bond issues in European countries usually are subject to a fiscal agency agreement, whereby a bank, often the bank acting as the principal paying agent for the issuer, is responsible for the interests of the bond holders, but as an agent of the issuer rather than as a trustee for the bondholders. International bond issues subject to UK governing law may be made under a trust

deed. An organization is appointed as trustee for the bondholders, and represents their interests in any dealings with the issuer.

A bank will agree to lead-manage an international bond issue only if the issuer agrees to have the issue credit rated. The issuer is vetted by one or more independent and internationally recognized vetting agencies, for example Moody's or Standard & Poor's, that gives the issue a credit rating according to its view about whether the issuer will have the ability to sustain the interest payments and eventually repay the principal at maturity. The rating will affect the pricing of the issue. Bonds that are not given an investment grade rating such as junk bonds or high-yield bonds, must be given either a high-coupon or a low-issue price to compensate investors for the high risk attached to the investment.

Bought Deal
A bought deal is now uncommon. It is a bond issue arrangement in which a single bank takes on the entire bond issue. Instead of forming an underwriting group and syndicating the issue, banks bid competitively to buy the bonds. The successful bank takes the whole issue on to its books, hoping to resell as quickly and as profitably as possible.

Issuing Government Bonds

Government bonds can be issued either on the international market and placed with investors, or issued on the domestic market. If the country has a strong domestic capital market, most government borrowing takes the form of domestic issues, for example in the US, European Union countries, Japan and Australia.

Summary

New issues raise capital for the issuer, but a liquid secondary market is a vital factor in creating investor interest. However, key considerations for both issuers and investors are:

- the issue price and expected returns for investors
- the method of issue, for example placements are targeted at institutional investors, but usually are quicker and less costly than a public offering
- the timing of the issue, and
- the success of the issue. Issuers can make sure of their money by getting the issue underwritten. However, a failure to attract end-investors will keep the price of the security depressed in its secondary market and make a subsequent new issue by the issuer more difficult to arrange.

7

Dealing

Procedures and systems for dealing in securities in the secondary market vary between individual markets, and also within the same market according to the type of security being traded. In any stock market, however, there are two important elements in buying or selling securities:

- bringing buyers and sellers together, and
- enabling them to obtain the best available price for buying or selling.

In an order-driven market, buy orders and sell orders are input to a central market place, perhaps an electronic order book, and if there is sufficient supply and demand, orders can be matched and transacted. In a quote-driven market, market makers maintain a secondary market by quoting continuous bid and offer prices for the shares in which they have agreed to make a market.

All investors need information about securities and transactions in securities in order to make sound investment decisions. The requirement for information therefore is highly significant.

Another significant aspect of dealing in securities is the need to protect investors, particularly non-professional investors, against dubious actions by intermediaries in the market.

Trading on a stock market is regulated by the market authorities. The real-time provision of information to the investing public and rules on investor protection are both elements of the regulations.

Although dealing procedures vary between different stock markets, it will be useful to look at some of the variations. This chapter looks briefly at trading systems on the New York Stock Exchange, Nasdaq, the London Stock Exchange and the international securities market.

Share Dealing on the New York Stock Exchange
Trading in shares is still conducted on the trading floor of the New York Stock Exchange building, although it is supported by powerful communications systems. Shares are traded by an auction process, and prices are set by supply and demand

Buy and sell orders for shares (stock) of a company listed on the NYSE are brought to an assigned location on the trading floor of the exchange. There are seventeen trading posts on the trading floor, each manned by a specialist and a team of clerks. Every listed security is traded in a unique location at one of these posts, where computer screen data about the security is continually available.

There are also about 1,500 trading booths around the edge of the trading floor, manned by floor brokers.

Orders to buy or sell shares come to the trading floor in one of two ways.

- A member firm of the exchange may send orders electronically to the specialist through the NYSE Superdot communication system. The specialist then acts as an agent for the order in the trading crowd at the trading location for the shares.
- Orders may come to floor brokers at their trading booth, by telephone or electronically, via the Broker Booth Support System. Once a broker receives an order, he or she act as its agent in the trading crowd.

Due to the strength of supply and demand, orders are transacted quickly.

NYSE Dealing: Specialist System

A trade will go through the following stages:

- An investor places a buy or sell order for shares in a NYSE-listed company with his brokerage firm.
- The brokerage firm maintains a stock account for the client, and will check the client's account to ensure that the order can be accepted. The broker will ask for the order details and key these into its order processing system. The order is transmitted to the trading floor of the NYSE, usually by computer link, but possibly by telephone.
- The Common Message Switch/Superdot system at the NYSE will, depending on the details of the order, either route the order to a floor broker's booth or directly to the trading post specialist for that stock.
- If the order is routed to the specialist, it appears on the specialist's display book screen. Orders routed to a floor broker appear on the broker's screen in the booth. The specialist or the broker then transacts the order at the trading location for the

stock. A broker will compete with other brokers to make the trade at the best price obtainable in a competitive auction process.

- Once the transaction has been made, a transaction report is sent back to the brokerage firm that initiated the order. The brokerage firm usually receives the transaction report within seconds of initiating the order.
- The brokerage firm processes the transaction report, crediting or debiting the stock account of the client with the number of shares bought or sold.
- A trade confirmation report is sent to the investor, who is required to submit a payment for any shares purchased.

Settlement of NYSE trades is three days after the day on which the trade was made (T + 3). Payment for purchased stock must be available for payment to the seller within three working days.

Transactions on Nasdaq

The Nasdaq stock market does not have a trading floor. The market is really a large inter-connected group of intermediaries and trading systems. It is a screen-based market with participants working from terminals in their offices. Unlike the New York Stock Exchange, Nasdaq does not operate with single specialists for each stock. Instead, several market participants each trade the stocks of a company through a computer network linking them to client investors and brokers around the world.

There are two types of market participant in Nasdaq:

- market makers and
- electronic communications networks (ECNs).

Market makers are independent dealers who compete for orders by displaying continuous bid and offer prices for the stock. They each have access to the Nasdaq computerized trading system. There are four categories of market maker.

- Retail market makers have a retail brokerage network, and handle orders from individual investors.
- Institutional market makers specialize in executing large block orders for institutional clients.
- Regional market-making firms specialize in both companies and investors in a particular geographical region, hoping to gain business through their specialized local knowledge and contacts.
- Wholesale market-making firms that trade shares on behalf of institutional clients and broker dealers who are not registered Nasdaq market makers. Wholesale market makers also can be an important source for the purchase of stock by other types of market maker.

ECNs are private electronic trading systems, first incorporated into Nasdaq in 1997. They operate both independently, matching buy and sell orders in an electronic order book in the system, and with a link to Nasdaq, where unmatched buy or sell orders might be traded instead. To trade on Nasdaq, an ECN must be certified with the Securities and Exchange Commission in the US and registered with Nasdaq. Examples of ECNs linked to Nasdaq are Archipelago, Instinet and Island.

When a market maker uses an ECN to represent an order, the order is first routed through the ECN to check for a match, and if no match is found, it is posted electronically in the Nasdaq system as an ECN quote. The order will be either executed on Nasdaq or matched and transacted with a new order coming through the ECN itself.

Market makers compete for orders and because they operate a quote-driven system, they will transact immediately any buy or sell order coming to them, and deal at their quoted price. Then they will seek the other side of the transaction to balance their position. For example, if they buy stock from an investor, they will seek another investor to sell it on to, perhaps by adjusting their quoted offer price. Also they can interact with market orders brought to Nasdaq through ECNs or broker-dealers.

Trading information is broadcast to users of Nasdaq through computer terminals worldwide. All Nasdaq participants have equal access to this information.

Example: Executing a Nasdaq Order

Suppose that an investor, Alpha, wants to buy 1,000 shares in XYZ Corporation. A call will be made to a broker who will check prices being quoted for the stock and transact the order with the market maker quoting the lowest offer price. Alternatively, the order might be initiated online, through the internet, in which case Alpha would have an online trading account, and would place the order through an online broker. The order then would be executed by either a market maker or an ECN at the best current price.

Instead of placing a simple market order asking the broker to make a transaction at the best available price, Alpha might have placed a limit order. A limit order specifies a maximum purchase price or minimum sale price an investor will accept for the shares.

Suppose that Alpha placed an order to buy 1,000 shares in XYZ Corporation, but at a price not exceeding 10 3/8 ($10.375) – Nasdaq quotes prices in sixteenths of a dollar. If the best price available is only 10 ¾, the order will not be executed. A market maker must deal with Alpha at that price, execute the order, or transmit the order to an ECN where it can be matched. However, if no market maker is willing to deal at this price, Alpha's price will become the most favorable quoted bid price on the market, and it will be displayed on the trading screen for all market participants to see. Someone wishing to sell 1,000 XYZ Corporation shares can make the deal with Alpha at 10 3/8.

Dealing on the London Stock Exchange

There are two main dealing systems for shares on the London Stock Exchange, and another system for dealing in government bonds (gilts).

Dealing in shares of the largest companies is order-driven, using an electronic order book system called SETS. Shares in second-tier companies are traded through a quote-driven system called SEAQ. In

February 2001, settlement of share transactions on the London Stock Exchange was changed to three days after trade date (T + 3). Previously, settlement had been on T + 5, and the change brought London into line with other major stock markets around the world such as NYSE and Nasdaq.

SETS

SETS is the London Stock Exchange Electronic Trading System that was introduced in 1997. Using SETS, investors place orders through a broker or broker dealer for inclusion in the electronic order book. Orders remain on the order book until a counterparty is found at the desired price, until the order is deleted, or until the order reaches its expiry time or date when it is removed from the order book without having been transacted. Once they are on the order book, orders are transacted automatically.

Only member firms of the London Stock Exchange or SETS participants may input orders or execute against existing orders on the order book. Non-members cannot access the order book directly, and must use a member firm or SETS participant as intermediary to carry out trades.

The order book is used for shares in the UK's largest companies, those companies that make up the FTSE 100, plus FTSE 100 reserve stocks, stocks in the Eurotop 300 Index and shares for which options are traded on LIFFE. In addition, if a company moves out of the FTSE 100, its shares continue to be traded on the SETS order book.

The SETS order book is based on an order-matching system in which member firms display their bid (buying) and offer (selling) orders to the market on an electronic order book that is in fact a list of bid and offer orders waiting to be transacted. Very large orders, however, are often transacted off the order book, for example by telephone.

Participants add orders or execute against existing orders by sending electronic messages to the system. Executions occur automatically in accordance with strict price and time priority, so that investors can be confident that their orders will be executed fairly.

Non-SETS securities: SEAQ

For most non-SETS securities, trading is done through SEAQ or by negotiation. Market makers are obliged to display to the market, throughout the trading day for all of the shares in which they make a market, their bid and offer prices, and the maximum transaction size to which these prices relate. Prices for larger transactions are subject to negotiation. Market makers compete to offer the best quote for the shares in which they make a market.

SEAQ (Stock Exchange Automated Quotation) is a quote-driven system for most UK listed companies, that distributes information about market-makers' bid and offer prices to the market. Registered market makers must maintain quoted prices during a mandatory quote period, and prices can be viewed on a number of screen-based information services such as Reuters and Bloomberg.

SEAQ identifies at any moment in the trading day, from an investor's point of view, the best available bid and offer prices, known as the touch, for every SEAQ security, and it also identifies by code name up to four market makers quoting this price. Other market makers' names and quotes also can be viewed on the screen.

Dealing in Gilts

In the London gilts market, there are specialized market makers, known as Gilt-Edged Market Makers or GEMMS. They do not have to quote firm bid and offer prices however, only indicative prices.

GEMMS often have to buy gilts from another market maker. Transactions between GEMMs are not made directly between buyer and seller, but anonymously via an inter-dealer broker (IDB).

A GEMM could sell gilts to a client that it does not yet have, in other words it could go short in the stock, and then would have to purchase stock to fulfill the order on settlement day. As an alternative to buying stock, it could borrow the stock that it needs for settlement from a Stock Exchange Money Broker (SEMB).

Dealing in Gilts

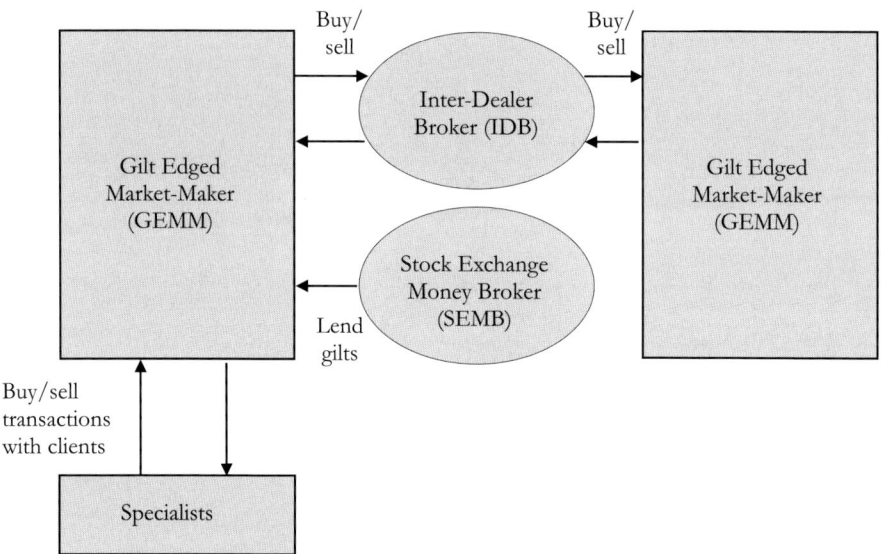

Negotiated Deals

Most *institutional business* in shares in the US and the UK is transacted off screen or off market and at different prices from those shown on trading screens. This is because many transactions by institutional investors such as pension funds, etc., are so large that they need to be the subject of individual negotiation between the institution or the institution's representative and the market participant trading the stock.

Dealing in International Bonds

Banks that lead-manage an international bond issue usually will undertake to maintain a secondary market in the bonds, and other banks also might act as broker-dealers for the bonds.

A major problem with transactions in international bonds is the cross-border nature of the transactions. A bondholder in one country might use a bank in another country to sell to an investor in a third country. The buyer and seller may hold their bonds with Clearstream or Euroclear, and wish to settle through them.

The secondary market in international securities is regulated by the International Securities Market Association, and its members use a system called Trax for matching and confirmation of trades, and for trade reporting.

Transactions are negotiated, often by telephone, although ISMA has introduced Coredeal, an electronic trading system.

Summary

Because dealing procedures vary between markets, it is not possible to specify the procedures for every stock market. However, the key issues in secondary market dealing are:

- liquidity, and a system whereby investors can buy or sell securities readily, at a fair price, wherever they want to
- intermediaries who are prepared to maintain a liquid market, dealing on their own account as necessary
- availability of price information to all market users so that they can obtain a fair price for buying or selling stock
- efficiency in transacting orders and in order processing (clearing and settlement)
- regulation by the market authorities, or self-regulation by market participants to ensure that a fair and orderly market is maintained.

8

Clearing and Settlement

Clearing and settlement are referred to as the back-office procedures in a securities transaction. All transactions must be cleared and settled.

- Clearing is the process by which a buyer and seller confirm the details of the transaction they have agreed, and the transaction is prepared for settlement.
- Settlement involves the actual payment by the buyer for the securities purchased, and the delivery by the seller to the buyer or the buyer's broker of the securities that have been sold.

Clearing and settlement systems vary between different markets.

Confirmation

Confirmation is the process whereby each party to a transaction checks and agrees its details.

When a transaction is arranged off-exchange by telephone between two firms of institutional investors, or between a dealer and an investment institution, the buyer and the seller will exchange messages in which they specify the details of the transaction they believe they have made. The details are then checked, and if the buyer and seller's details correspond, they will exchange confirmations. Once confirmation has taken place, each party will take the necessary steps to settle the transaction on the settlement date.

The confirmation of transactions made by telephone can be a slow and error-prone operation. In the past, it was by no means uncommon for

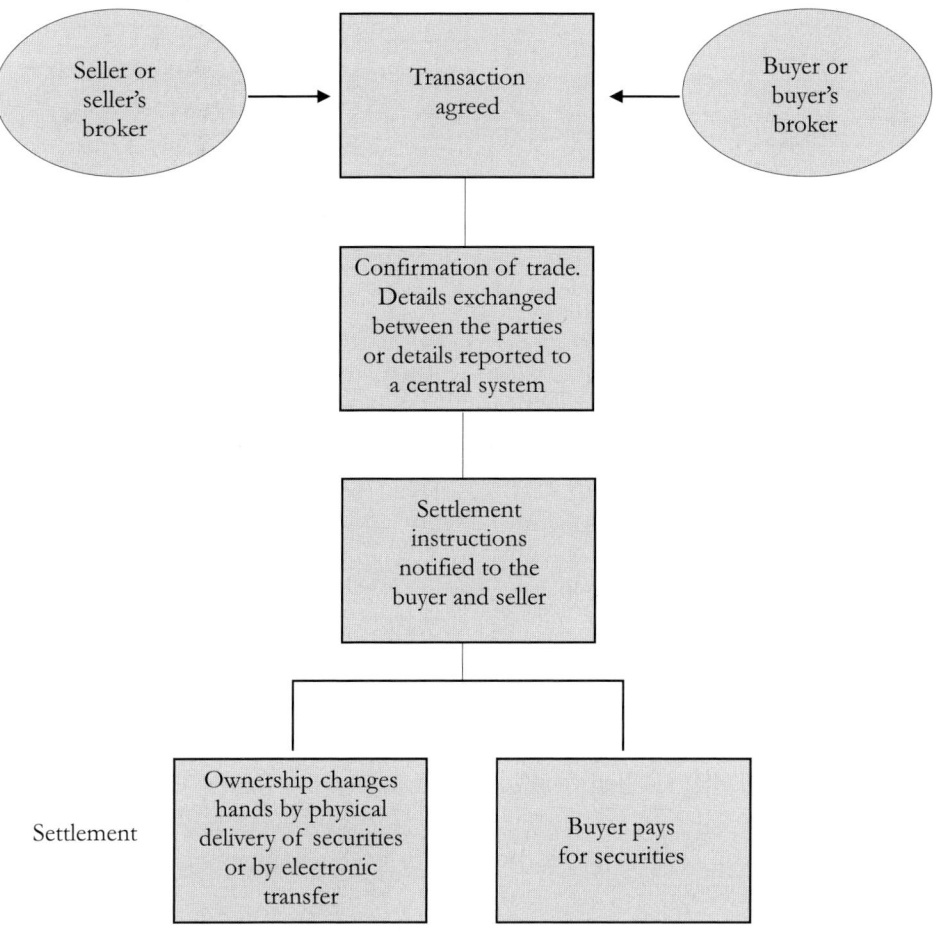

buyer and seller to disagree on the details, such as the quantity of the security being traded, the price, or even who was the buyer and who was the seller.

Improvements in confirmation were made by the introduction of computer systems. After a transaction has been agreed, buyer and seller may be required to input details of the bargain into a clearing system. This will look for a match for each item input, and when it matches the input of the buyer with the input of the seller, it reports a confirmation of the bargain. Unmatched items are notified back to the parties that input them, to be sorted out between them.

The International Securities Market Association (ISMA) has operated a computerized order-matching and confirmation system, known as Trax, since 1992, for secondary market transactions in the international securities markets. As well as providing a confirmation service, Trax also acts as a trade-reporting system, bringing greater immediacy and openness in price information in the international bond market. Before Trax was introduced, international bond dealers gave indicative prices at the end of each day, and prices available to the market were less immediate and less specific.

When using electronic trading through an order book, orders are matched automatically within the system, and transaction reports are sent to the buyer and the seller.

Novation

In some securities markets, an organization acting on behalf of the stock exchange steps between the buyer and seller in every transaction, and becomes the seller to the buyer and the buyer to the seller. The seller's contractual obligations are to the exchange, and the exchange guarantees that the buyer's side of the transaction will be carried out. Similarly, the buyer's obligations are to the exchange, and the exchange guarantees that the seller's contractual obligations will be carried out.

This process is known as novation.

Novation

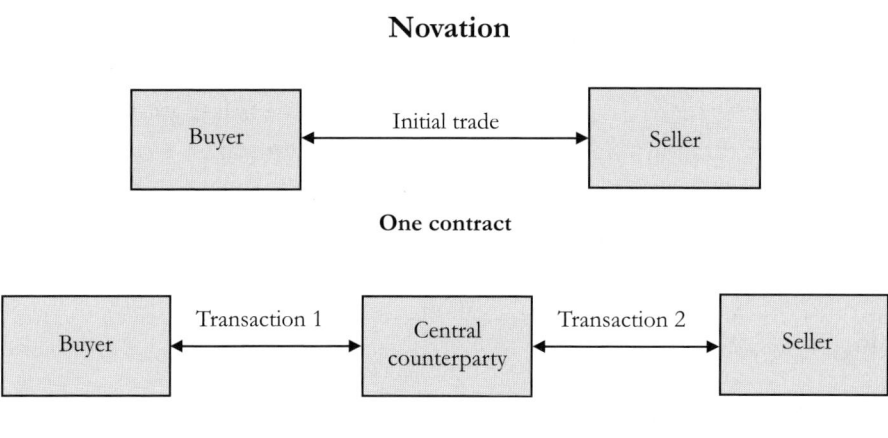

Two contracts

When the exchange, or an organization acting on its behalf, becomes the other party to the transaction for both the seller and the buyer, it can organize the settlement process. It can instruct the seller on making the appropriate quantity of the securities available for transfer to the buyer on settlement date and notify the seller on the payment that will be made into its bank account. It also can instruct the buyer how much will be required in payment on settlement date, and to where the payment should be made.

Another consequence of novation, and the exchange acting as a central counterparty to all transactions, is that all firms of market makers or broker dealers can settle all their transactions on any one day by means of a single payment to or from the central counterparty. A broker-dealer might make several hundreds or even thousands of transactions for settlement on one day, but all can be settled by one payment. This is a process known as netting.

Preparing for Settlement

Once a transaction has been confirmed, the buyer and seller must each make preparations for settlement on the appointed settlement date.

Where transactions are matched and confirmed by a central securities depository instructions for settlement are issued by the CSD. The buyer's bank can be notified of the necessary payment details, and arrangements can be made for the transfer of the shares from the seller's to the buyer's book entry stock account.

Settlement

Stock markets have an order cycle, and settlement must take place within a specified time of the trade being made. Under the terms of real-time gross settlement, payment and delivery of securities must be immediate, when the transaction is made. Many stock markets work to a cycle of settlement three days after the trade date (T + 3 settlement). This is applied in the US, for example, and was introduced by the London Stock Exchange in 2001.

When investors have accounts with a central securities depository, they also are required to have a bank account with a bank that has a link to the clearing system of the CSD. Payment instructions are sent to the buyer's bank, and a notification of payments receivable is sent to the seller's bank. The bank is then responsible for ensuring that its client will have sufficient money in its account on any day for the net settlement of its securities transactions.

Some buyers of securities will want the securities in certificate form. Equally, the seller may be selling shares for which there are certificates rather than a book entry in a CSD system. The settlement process may also involve:

- the surrender of the certificate by the seller, or
- the production of a certificate for the buyer.

The seller of a bearer security will transfer ownership to the buyer simply by surrendering the certificate. The seller of registered shares in certificate form will surrender the certificate to the buyer's broker, but the certificate will then be surrendered to the registrar for the company.

The registrar will be required to produce a new registered certificate for the buyer having registered the transfer of ownership in the share register. If the certificate is for more shares than the seller has sold, the registrar also will produce a certificate for the balance remaining of the seller's shares for dispatch to the seller.

Payment

Payment for transactions should be made on or before settlement date. Because a money payment is a banking transaction, the actual transfer of funds takes place outside the settlement system of the stock market. A broker dealer issues a contract note to a client, showing the amount payable or receivable, and the settlement date.

Clearing and Settlement in the US: the DTCC

As an illustrative example of an advanced clearing and settlement system, it may be useful to conclude this chapter by looking at the role of the Depository Trust and Settlement Corporation (DTCC).

The DTCC was founded in 1999 by the merger of the Depository Trust Company (DTC) and the National Securities Clearing Corporation (NSCC). The DTC and NSCC continue to perform different functions, but within one overall organization.

Between them, the DTC and NSCC provide an infrastructure for the clearing and settlement of most transactions in equities, corporate bonds and municipal bonds in the US, and for the custody of these securities mainly in electronic book entry form.

The DTC is a securities depository, and a clearing house for transactions. Institutional investors hold their securities with the DTCC in book entry form. The DTC also handles payments of dividends and interest on behalf of its participants. The role of the DTC is similar to the functions carried out by CSDs such as Clearstream, Euroclear and Crest.

The NSCC processes almost all broker-to-broker trades in the US in equities, corporate bonds and municipal bonds. It provides a centralized clearance and settlement service, and once a transaction has been confirmed, it acts as a central counterparty, through novation, for the buyer and the seller. Settlement of transactions is through the NSCC that arranges settlement by netting.

Broker-to-Broker Trade

A broker-to-broker trade in shares or bonds will be cleared and settled as follows:

- A buyer of securities and a seller each instruct their broker on the order they wish to transact. The trade is made in the marketplace, on the NYSE or Nasdaq, where the orders of the buyer and seller are matched and executed.
- On trade day, the transaction details are transmitted from the exchange to the NSCC. Most transactions in shares are already locked in, meaning that the transaction has been confirmed within the market place (stock market) and both sides of the trade are submitted to the NSCC. For most bond trades, each broker submits trade details to the NSCC separately, and the matching and confirmation are carried out by the NSCC.
- NSCC processes and records the transaction. On T + 1, it issues T contracts for the locked-in equity trades, and issues reports on bond trades submitted directly by brokers. The documents issued by NSCC confirm that the transaction is ready for settlement, and that the NSCC has assumed responsibility for settlement. The seller and buyer are now contractually liable to NSCC.
- NSCC instructs the DTC to move the securities being sold to the NSCC's account within the DTC system, and on settlement from the NSCC account to the buying broker's account within the system. The DTC will transfer securities between accounts electronically, by book entry transfer.
- On T + 2, NSCC issues to each broker a summary of all the transactions carried out by that broker that are due for settlement on T + 3. NSCC has a Continuous Net Settlement

system for brokers, and settlement each day between NCC and each broker is by means of a single net payment, from NSCC to the broker or from the broker to NSCC.

- NSCC issues money-settlement instructions to the settlement bank of both the buyer's broker and the seller's broker. It also gives its own bank payment instructions for T + 3.
- Settlement is on T + 3. The securities are transferred within the DTC to the account of the buyer's broker. The net payments between NSCC and the brokers is by the Fedwire service, a same-day electronic funds transfer service.

9

Market Regulation

Every capital market, to a greater or lesser degree, is regulated. Regulation is needed to protect market participants and to provide an orderly market with established rules of behavior. Investors need protection against malpractice by issuers or market intermediaries. Non-professional investors (private individuals) need more protection than institutional investors, who might have better access to market information.

All participants in the market have to follow established procedures and methods so that transactions can be carried out with the sure knowledge of the responsibilities of each party. Knowing what everyone else will do brings orderliness, removes uncertainty and helps the market to function more effectively.

Regulators

The regulators in a capital market may be an agency of the government, or possibly a self-regulating organization of market participants.

The government establishes the framework for its country's capital markets by:

- specifying, through criminal and civil law, market behavior that is illegal or actionable
- in some cases, imposing restrictions on the inflow of foreign capital or the outflow of capital and dividends from the country

- providing a tax regime within which capital markets operate
- creating a legal structure for the regulation of the markets.

Objectives of Regulation

An agency of government or a self-regulating organization has specific regulatory objectives. These are:

- to maintain confidence in the national financial system
- public/consumer awareness
- the protection of consumers, and
- the reduction of financial crime.

The *public awareness* objective is to promote public understanding of the financial system, and in particular it includes:

- promoting awareness of both the benefits and the risks associated with different kinds of investment and financial dealing, and
- providing appropriate information and advice.

The *protection of consumers* objective is to secure an appropriate degree of protection for consumers. In broad terms, a consumer is someone who uses the services of a market professional for a securities transaction or other type of financial transaction.

Financial crime includes any offence involving fraud or dishonesty, misconduct in a financial market, the misuse of information relating to a financial market and handling the proceeds of crime (money laundering).

What is Regulated?

A market regulator will issue rules and codes of conduct, and possibly principles of market conduct. It also will enforce any government statutes that apply to securities markets activity.

A regulatory body establishes rules for who is permitted to trade in the market, and could, if necessary, expel members from the right to trade.

It also might be responsible for admitting new issues shares and bonds to the official list.

A stock exchange will regulate the conduct and activities of its members. However, it will regulate only those aspects of exchange activities that are not already subject to regulation by the government's regulatory body. For example, a stock exchange will issue regulations on the settlement cycle, and on the reporting of information about trades to the exchange, for public disclosure.

What Can Go Wrong?

It is worth considering some of the problems with which regulation is designed to deal. It may be easier to understand a rule if its purpose is known.

Investments
- Worthless securities could be sold as if they had a value.
- Securities could be issued with hidden terms and conditions.
- Investors might be unaware of the risks involved in their investments.
- Directors of companies could misuse funds entrusted to them by investors.
- New issues of securities could be made with inadequate or misleading information.

Dealing
- One party to a transaction could know something that the other party does not, and seeks to profit from this inside knowledge. Insider dealing is a criminal offence in many countries, but is difficult to prove.
- The price or terms of a deal might not be to the best advantage of the investor, but in some way fixed by the intermediary.
- The market as a whole could be rigged by concerted buying or

selling by a group of dealers to affect the price.

Takeovers
- Misleading information could be published to influence shareholders to accept or reject a takeover bid.
- The market could be manipulated to change the relative attractiveness of a takeover involving a share-for-share offer in which the purchaser tries to buy a target company by paying with a new issue of its shares, for example by boosting artificially the share price of the purchasing company.

Settlement
- Securities or payment may not be delivered in time on settlement date.
- Securities or payment may not be delivered at all, perhaps because the other party (buyer or seller) or an intermediary (broker or dealer) is insolvent.

This list of problems is not exhaustive. Other misdemeanors could occur against which a government and market authorities should seek to offer protection, especially to investors. However, the list does suggest why extensive regulation might be desirable.

Regulation in the US: an Outline

In the US, the main agency for regulating the domestic capital markets in securities is the Securities and Exchange Commission (SEC). Banking is regulated at a federal level by the Federal Reserve Board, and regulation of the financial futures and options markets is the responsibility of the Commodity Futures Trading Commission. When securities are issued and traded within a single state's boundaries, the market is subject to state government regulation, not the SEC.

There is also self-regulation in some individual exchanges such as the New York Stock Exchange, and by professional organizations such as the National Association of Securities Dealers and the Securities Industry Association.

Glass-Steagall Act

The Glass-Steagall Act (Banking Act 1933) barred commercial banks from involvement in securities trading and underwriting, either directly or through an investment bank subsidiary. The aim of the act was to protect traditional deposit banking from the risks of losses in securities trading, as well as to protect depositors and the banking system. Until the 1980s, commercial and investment banking activities were rigidly segregated by the Federal Reserve.

The Glass-Steagall Act was re-interpreted in the late 1980s, and the Federal Reserve has authorized some commercial banks to set up holding companies, with separate directorships and funding, that can operate investment-banking subsidiaries.

Brief History of Regulation of the London Stock Market

At one time, the London stock market was self-regulatory. The origins of the London stock market were in the coffee-houses of London in the seventeenth century, where people met to raise and invest money in commercial ventures. The way in which the London market has been regulated developed unevenly from these informal beginnings. To begin with, the regulator was the owner of the coffee-house, if he did not like a person, or thought he was crooked and so would damage the reputation of the house, he would not be allowed a seat.

From this developed the concept of self-regulation. It was in the interests of market members that investors should have confidence in the market. One member's bad practise damaged the business for all. The LSE members made the market's rules themselves, and policed them. The ultimate sanction was expulsion from the market.

To some extent self-regulation can be satisfactory. It could be argued that those who operate the market are the best judges of good and bad practise; it is in their interests to preserve the reputation of the whole operation. On the other hand, it could become a club, where insiders protect each other and prevent external competition and investigations.

Over time, government regulation has increased. A Financial Services Act was introduced in 1986, setting up a governmental regulatory body for the financial markets. This body, now called the Financial Services Authority, has been given further powers by the Financial Services and Markets Act 2000. With few exceptions, self-regulation of the markets in the UK is non-existent.

Participants in the capital markets must be recognized and given authority to operate by the FSA. The FSA also is responsible for issuing and enforcing codes of practise for market participants. It is responsible for policing activities in the markets, and for enforcing the law on insider dealing, market abuse, and money laundering. It has responsibility for the listing rules, with which companies with shares or other securities on the official list must comply. It is responsible for enforcing rules of conduct by company directors in the stock market, in particular the rules restricting the times when directors may buy or sell shares in their company, to prevent them benefiting from their special inside knowledge of the company's performance.

The UK legislation also provides for the recognition of exchanges by the Financial Service Authority. There is a large number of recognized exchanges, including the London Stock Exchange, LIFFE, Nasdaq and, for the international bond market, the ISMA.

Regulation of the International Capital Markets

There is no single regulatory authority for the international capital markets. Market participants are subject to differing regulations, according to the country within which they are based. Each country has different rules and tax laws for securities trading abroad by its residents. The absence of a single controlling body helps to explain the growth of the international markets, in which investors and issuers could experiment with new and varied financial instruments, free from restrictions preventing their development. In the absence of a single controlling body or regulator, self-regulation and self-monitoring becomes essential to preserve a market's reputation for integrity and honest dealing.

The international bond market has two self-regulatory bodies, the International Securities Market Association (ISMA) and its associated group, the International Primary Market Association.

ISMA regulates the conduct and practises of members, polices the market and provides a conciliation service for disputes between members. As a collective body, ISMA also has been active in standardizing market procedures, and helping to improve settlement procedures for market transactions.

The international capital markets also operate through some national stock exchanges, such as the London Stock Exchange and the Luxembourg Stock Exchange. These exchanges provide a listing for a number of international equities and bonds.

Summary

Greater regulation to protect investors should encourage more investment. Arguably, however, *excessive* regulation could damage the efficiency and costs of the market, perhaps resulting in a shift of investment activity to an alternative market, for example from a domestic market to another country's domestic market, or to the international market.

10

Risk Management and the Capital Markets

All participants in the capital markets must accept some risk. This risk should be properly managed. Risk arises from the possibility of a loss occurring, directly or indirectly, as a consequence of making a transaction or taking a financial or investment position.

Capital Market Risks

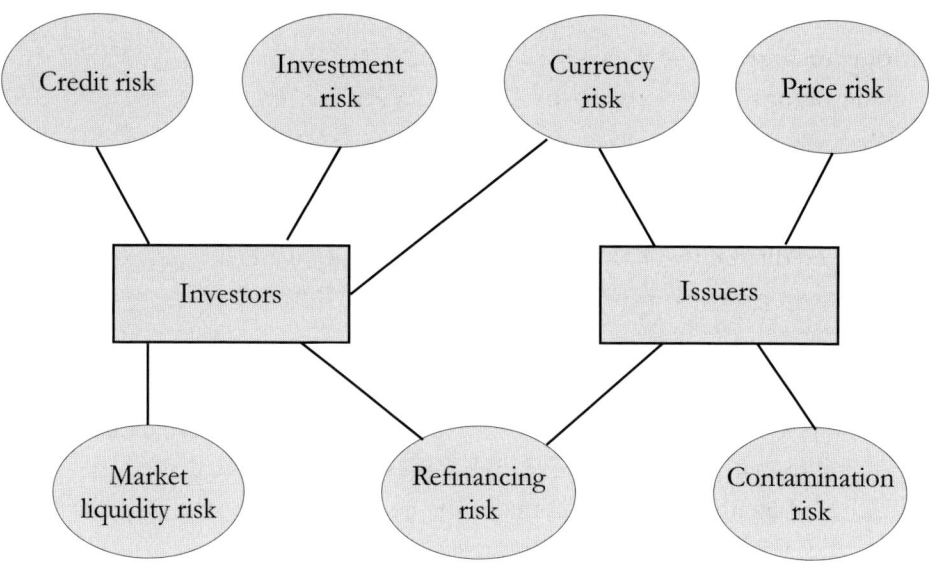

Risks for the Investor

Investors can be exposed to the greatest risk. They can suffer losses from unfair or dishonest dealings by issuers of securities, intermediaries and other investors. The purpose of market regulation, as explained in Chapter 9, is to protect investors from such activities.

The risks for an investor include:

- credit risk and counterparty risk
- investment risk
- currency risk
- market liquidity risk
- refinancing risk.

Credit Risk

Credit risk arises from the possibility that an issuer of securities will fail to pay amounts owed to investors, either in full or on time. This risk applies principally to holders of bonds or preferred stock. The interest or preference dividend might not be paid on schedule, and in the case of bonds, the issuer could fail to repay the debt principal at maturity.

Some reassurance about credit risk for debt securities is provided by credit ratings. Agencies such as Moody's, Standard & Poor's and Fitch IBCA will give a debt issue a rating to indicate, in the agency's view, the probability that interest payments and the principal repayment will be made in full and on time. Investors can choose to avoid debt securities with a credit rating below a certain level, for example below an investment grade rating.

Counterparty Risk

Counterparty risk, in the context of stock-market transactions, is the possibility that the other party to the transaction will fail to carry out his/her obligations at settlement, and either will fail to pay for purchased securities or fail to deliver the securities he/she has sold.

Investment Risk

Investment risk, or price risk, is the risk of a fall in the value of an investment. If a bond issuer is a company that goes into liquidation, the full investment could be at risk. More commonly investments could lose value in the secondary market.

- The market value of debt securities will fall if current market rates of interest go up. Share prices also are likely to fall when interest rates go up because shareholders, like investors in debt, will expect a higher return from their investments.

- A share price also can fall whenever the market revises downwards its expectations of the company's future profits and dividends. When a company issues a profits warning, the collapse in the share price can be very substantial.

Most investments carry the risk that the actual returns will be less than the expected returns. When the perceived risk of poor returns is higher, investors will demand a higher yield on their investment, as compensation for the risk.

Some investors could take on risk, speculating on a future rise or fall in market prices in the hope of making a large profit. However, speculators can trade in options or futures rather than in the shares themselves, i.e. in the cash markets.

Currency Risk

Currency risk arises for investors in securities denominated in a foreign currency. If the currency falls in value against the investor's domestic currency, the market value of the investment in the investor's currency will fall and the investor will suffer a loss.

Example

Delta, a US investor, purchased UK government securities for £25 million in July when the sterling/dollar exchange rate was £1 = $1.60. By December, the market price of the securities was unchanged, but the exchange rate was £1 = $1.40.

Analysis

Delta purchased £25 million of gilts in July, when they were worth $40 million. By December, they were still worth £25 million, but the equivalent dollar value was just $35 million (25 million x 1.40). Delta has suffered a loss, in dollar terms, of $5 million because of the fall in the value of sterling against the dollar.

Investors normally are reluctant to buy foreign securities when they suspect that the currency is weak, and could fall in value. Some protection against long-term currency risk sometimes can be obtained by using currency swaps.

Market Liquidity Risk
Investors could face the risk of an illiquid secondary market for their securities, and could have difficulties selling their investments at a fair price whenever they wish. An investor wishing to sell securities but unable to find a ready buyer could:

- hold on to the securities and hope that a buyer eventually will be found, or
- reduce the price below a fair value in order to attract a buyer, and consequently receive less for the securities than they ought to be worth.

Market makers or broker dealers attempt to create a liquid secondary market in order to remove investors' concerns about this risk.

Refinancing Risk
Refinancing risk arises from the possibility that an issuer of securities could require new finance at a future time to avoid going into liquidation. Investors would then have the choice of supporting a new issue of securities to protect their existing investment, or to risk a complete loss in value of their investment when the company goes into liquidation. The risk could apply to investors in shares or debt securities, and to lending banks.

Example 1
Sierra, a large UK public company, has large debts and is making only low trading profits. Profits are insufficient to cover the payments of

interest on its debts. The company decides to make a one-for-four rights issue, to raise new equity capital. The money would be used to pay off some of the company's debts, reducing the interest costs and thereby making its financial position more secure.

Analysis
In this situation, a refinancing risk arises for the ordinary shareholders of Sierra, who must either:

- support the rights issue to enable the company to switch some of its funding from debt to equity, or
- risk the collapse of the company and the loss of their investment.

Example 2
Tango, a large public company, has $200 million of outstanding loans from a syndicate of banks that will mature within the next twelve months. It will be unable to make the principal payments, although it can meet the scheduled interest payments.

Analysis
The banks might agree to a refinancing package, giving Tango sufficient new loans to allow it to repay the maturing loans. The perceived credit risk from lending to Tango will be higher than when the original loans were made because Tango is unable to repay the loan principal. The banks will demand a higher margin on the new loans, for example 150 basis points above the London Interbank Offered Rate, compared with 50 basis points above LIBOR for the original loans.

Risks for the Issuer

There also are risks in the capital markets for issuers of securities. These can be kept under control by means of sound financial management, and by exercising judgment on the timing and pricing of issues, and in the choice of markets and securities for issue.

Risks for issuers include:

- price risk
- contamination risk
- refinancing risk
- currency risk

Price Risk

An issuer could fail to obtain the best price for an issue. The consequence would be higher interest costs when debt is being issued, or a bigger dilution in profits per share when equity is being issued.

The timing of issues can be very important. There could be a short window of opportunity during which favorable interest rates or share prices are obtainable. A change in interest rates also could make it better to issue securities either sooner or later, depending on whether interest rates go up or down.

Example 1

Victor, a large multinational company, wishes to raise $150 million from an international bond issue. Through an investment bank acting as lead manager, Victor issues ten-year bonds at an interest rate of 8%. Three months later, the same bonds could have been issued at 6%.

Analysis

If Victor had waited three months before making the issue, the annual interest cost would be 200 basis points (2%) per annum lower, giving an annual saving of $3 million.

Example 2

Romeo, a UK company, has 20 million shares in issue. To raise £20 million extra capital, Romeo plans a one-for-four rights issue at £4 per share. This compares with the current market price per share of £4.10. It is expected that the capital raised by the company will be used to increase earnings to £5 million.

Soon after the issue, growing market confidence sent share prices higher, and a one-for-five rights issue could have been made at £5 per share.

Analysis
The company issued five million new shares to raise £20 million. Earnings per share are expected to be:

$$\frac{£5,000,000}{25 \text{ million shares}} \quad = \quad 20 \text{ pence per share}$$

If the company had waited, however, and issued four million shares at £5 to raise the £20 million, earnings per share would be about 4% higher, at:

$$\frac{£5,000,000}{24 \text{ million shares}} \quad = \quad 20.83 \text{ pence per share}$$

Offers for sale and placements of new issues introduce the risk of under-pricing the issue. In a buoyant stock market, offers for sale by tender could be used to obtain a better price. In the case of government securities, an issue could be auctioned.

Contamination Risk
When one issue fails, or when a company incurs investor dissatisfaction with an existing issue, there is a risk that the success of future issues could be affected adversely by past failures. In a similar way, difficulties could be experienced with an issue in one particular market, affecting all other issuers in the same market. This is contamination risk.

A company could, for example, make a rights issue to raise new capital at an issue price of £4 per share. The issue could fail and be left in the hands of the underwriters. If the company wanted to raise still more capital in the future, it could be much more difficult to organize a rights issue because there would be a greater reluctance among underwriters to support it unless the issue price were heavily discounted to the current market price.

Refinancing Risk

An issuer of debt securities will expect to make interest and principal payments on schedule. The risk that it might not be able to, and be forced to seek refinancing, faces the issuer as well as investors. A company should seek to manage its financial structure and avoid the financial risks from over-borrowing (excessive financial gearing or leverage).

Currency Risk

The risk for a borrower with a foreign currency loan is that the currency of the loan could increase in value against the borrower's domestic currency. This could increase the cost for the borrower to service and repay the loan.

Example

A UK company borrowed €21 million when the exchange rate was £1 = €1.50, at an interest rate of 5% per annum. It converted the capital into sterling for domestic use.

Subsequently the exchange rate changed to £1 = €1.20, with sterling falling sharply in value against the euro.

Analysis

The company borrowed €21 million and converted this into £14 million in sterling at an exchange rate of £1 = €1.50.

Interest costs of €1.05 million per annum (5% of €21 million) will cost £875,000 at the new exchange rate of 1.20, compared with the expected cost of £700,000 when the exchange rate was 1.50.

The cost of repaying the loan at €1.20 will be £17.5 million (€21 million ÷ 1.20), £3.5 million more than the amount originally borrowed.

Conclusion

For investors and issuers in the capital markets, there are risks that have to be managed. For issuers, many of the risks can be controlled through sound financial management of the business, careful choice of markets and securities, and in the timing and pricing of issues.

Risks for the investor are unavoidable, except for investments in risk-free securities such as US Treasuries for US investors. Investors should expect a higher return for their investment risk, and will look for investments that provide a satisfactory balance between risk and return, with returns either in the form of regular income – interest and dividends, or capital gains – increases in the market value of the investments.

Glossary

ADR
American Depositary Receipt. Form in which shares of foreign companies usually are traded on US stock markets.

Ask Price
See Offer Price.

Auction
For primary issues of securities, it is a method of issue in which investors are invited to bid for securities. The highest bidders are allocated the securities, and must pay the price they bid. In secondary-market trading, auction means a system of trading in which prices are set by supply and demand, with orders that come to the market competing with each other for execution.

Bearer Security
Security for which possession of a certificate, or as evidenced in a book entry system) is sufficient evidence of ownership. In the case of certificated securities, dividend or interest coupons are attached to the certificate. To obtain payment, the coupon must be detached and presented to the issuer. Title to the securities is transferred by physical delivery of the certificate.

Bid Rate
Rate or price at which a market maker will buy a security.

BIS
Bank for International Settlements. A Swiss-based club for the central bankers of the main developed economies.

Bond

A negotiable long-term debt instrument. The issuer promises to pay the holder a fixed amount of principal at a specific future date (at maturity of the bond) and a series of interest payments. Long-term usually means over five years to maturity from the date of issue.

Book-Entry System

Computer system in which ownership of securities can be recorded in electronic form. Only participants or members of the system may hold securities in book-entry form. Other organizations or individuals wishing to hold their securities in book-entry form must do so by means of nominee accounts, maintained on their behalf by a participant in the system.

Bought Deal

Arrangement for an issue of debt securities whereby one institution buys the entire issue, and then resells the securities to other investors.

Broker

Person trading in a market on behalf of a client.

Broker-Dealer

Organization acting as a broker for clients and also dealing in securities on its own account. Broker-dealers often are instrumental in maintaining a liquid market in an order-driven trading system.

Bundare are

Government bond of the German goverment.

Central Securities Depository (CSD)

Organization that provides a book-entry system for holding securities to its members/participants, and which also provides a clearing service for transactions in securities. Examples of depository trust and clearing corporations are Clearstream, Euroclear, the DTCC (US) and Crest (UK).

Chartist (Technical Analyst)

Stock market analyst who attempts to predict future share price trends from an analysis of past price trends.

Clearing System

A system for the clearing of transactions in securities. Clearing may involve order matching and confirmation, and also will involve notifying buyers and sellers of securities what they must do to ensure that settlement takes place on the appointed settlement date. A clearing system also may provide a settlement service and a payment netting service.

Commercial Bank

A bank that takes deposits from customers and provides loans and money transmission services as a major part of its business.

Convertible Security

A security (bonds or preferred stock) giving its holder the right to exchange the security into ordinary shares of the company, at a stated rate of conversion, on a specified future date or during a specified future period.

Coupon

The interest rate, fixed or floating rate, paid on a bond or note, expressed as a percentage of its face value.

Credit Rating

Rating of creditworthiness, given to issues of both short-term and long-term debt securities. Credit ratings are graded, with a number of investment-grade ratings and some non-investment-grade ratings. Ratings are given by specialist agencies that are paid for their services by the debt issuer.

Debenture Stock

Loan stock issued under a debenture. A debenture is a written acknowledgment of a debt by a company, normally containing provisions as to interest payments, principal repayments and any security.

Derivative
A type of security, such as options, futures and swaps, that has evolved from instruments in the cash markets such as shares, bonds, foreign currency and loans, and, in part, derive their value from them.

Deutsche Börse
Organization operating the German stock markets.

Depository Trust and Clearing Corporation (DTCC)
Central securities depository, also providing clearing and settlement services for most transactions in US shares, and corporate and municipal bonds. The DTCC acts as the other counterparty for all trades, and so guarantees settlement to all buyers and sellers.

Electronic Communications Network (ECN)
Electronic trading system for dealing in securities. Some ECNs have links to Nasdaq, so that orders input to the ECN may be executed within Nasdaq.

Equity
A company's issued share capital, excluding preferred stock. Normally, the ordinary shares of the company.

Eurobond
A term for an international bond that is a bond issued simultaneously in several countries and subsequently traded internationally. The term is no longer common following the introduction of the euro and euro bonds that are bonds denominated in euros.

Eurodollar
A dollar placed in an account with a bank outside the US.

FRN
Floating rate note. Variable-rate debt security.

Fundamental Analysis
Method of assessing the appropriate market value of a security from

expectations of future dividends or interest, and a marginal investor's required yield on the investment.

Future

A standard exchange-traded instrument. Futures are traded on futures and options exchanges, and are contracts to buy or sell a standard quantity of an underlying item, often a notional item, for settlement at a future date. Futures are traded in a range of items, including bonds, share indices and shares of some individual companies.

Gilts

UK government bonds (gilt-edged stock).

Hybrid Instrument

Security that combines features of equity with features of debt securities.

Investment Bank

A bank that specializes in financial market activities rather than lending and money transmission.

IPMA

International Primary Market Association. Voluntary organization of institutions that operate as managing banks in international primary market issues.

ISMA

International Securities Market Association. Voluntary self-regulatory association of institutions that operate as intermediaries in the secondary market for international securities. Members of the IPMA are also members of ISMA.

LIBOR

London Interbank Offered Rate. Interest rate at which major London banks offer to lend short-term funds to other major banks. Rates are obtained from a number of leading banks by the British Bankers' Association, and published as a market average. LIBOR rates are published for a range of maturities, up to about 12 months, and for different currencies including dollar, sterling, euro, Swiss franc.

Listed Security
Security that is included in the official list of securities in a country.
Within the EU, the official list is maintained by an official listing
authority, in the UK this is the UK Listing Authority, a part of the
Financial Services Authority. A listed security will be traded on the main
market of the leading stock exchange in the country concerned.

Market Maker
Dealer in a quote-driven market willing to quote continuous two-way
prices (bid and offer prices) for securities and to trade in the securities at
those prices.

Matched Bargain
Transaction for which a buyer is, or has to be, found to purchase
securities that someone wishes to sell.

Naked Debenture
Term for unsecured loan stock.

Note
A medium-term debt security. Medium-term could be taken as two to
five years to maturity from the date of issue.

Offer Price
Rate or price at which a market maker will sell a security. Also called the
ask price.

Option (Share Option)
Instrument giving its holder the right to subscribe for an ordinary share
or a number of shares in a company at a fixed price, at a stated future
time. Options can be issued by companies to subscribe for new shares.
Traded options in shares are a different type of option, and are traded on
options exchanges.

Order-Driven Market
Market in which transactions activity is driven by orders to buy or sell

coming into the market. Distinct from a quote-driven market. Examples of order-driven markets are the New York Stock Exchange and any stock market that uses an electronic order book for trading.

Over-the-Counter (OTC) Market
Market in which dealing is by telephone rather than on an exchange.

Placing (Placement)
New issue of securities sold to a small number of investors without being offered to the general investing public.

Primary Market
Market for new issues of securities.

Prospectus
Offer document accompanying a proposed new issue of securities, containing details of the issue and the issuer, and inviting investors to subscribe.

Public Offering
Primary issue of securities, in which the securites are offered to the general investing public.

Quote-Driven Market
Market in which transactions activity is driven by the continual availability of two-way prices from market makers who are willing to deal at those prices. Distinct from an order-driven market.

Real Time Gross Settlement (RTGS)
Settlement of a transaction in securities when the transaction takes place. Used, for example, for the settlement of transactions in Japanese Government Bonds (JGBs) on the Tokyo Stock Exchange.

Registered Security
Security for which evidence of ownership is maintained on a register. When certificates are issued, each contains the name of the owner. Dividends or interest are paid to the name and address on the register.

Title cannot be transferred without the signed consent of the owner or nominee.

SEC
Securities and Exchange Commission. Regulatory body for the US securities markets.

Secondary Market
Market in which securities are bought and sold once they have been issued.

Security
A negotiable debt or equity or hybrid obligation, commonly evidenced by a certificate.

Settlement
In the context of a transaction in securities, the payment for the securities by the buyer and the delivery of the securities to the buyer by the seller. Ideally, delivery and payment happen at the same time. Transactions on a stock market must be settled a specific number of days after the trade date, for example on $T + 3$, three working days after the day the transaction was made, although some transactions are settled on the same day as the trade is made.

Shelf Registration
A method of registering a new issue of securities in advance with the stock market authorities, and having most of the documentation pre-prepared and approved. A new issue of securities is then available off-the-shelf, with only a small amount of additional documentation required.

Swap
An agreement in which two parties undertake to exchange a stream of payments, usually at regular intervals, over a period of time that can be ten years or longer. In an interest-rate swap, payments of interest on a notional amount of principal are exchanged. In a currency swap, there is

an exchange of both principal and interest in one currency for interest and principal in a second currency.

Syndicated Loan
A large loan from several banks together to a single borrower.

Tap Stock
Government bonds issued to the market over a period of time when demand exists, and usually in irregular amounts.

Technical Analyst
See Chartist.

Treasuries
US government debt securities (Treasury bonds, notes and bills).

Uncertificated Security
Security held in electronic book-entry form, without the existence of a share or bond certificate.

Underwriter
Organization that for a percentage commission agrees to purchase a quantity of unsold securities in a new issue, at the issue price, if there are insufficient other buyers.

Warrant (Share Warrant)
Instrument giving its holder the right to subscribe for a stated amount of new shares in a company at a fixed price, on or after a given date. Usually issued in association with loan stock.

Zero Coupon Bond
Bond that pays no interest, issued at a deep discount to par value and redeemed at par.

Index